Testimonials

"So often when we think about finance in our society, we don't take into account the importance of arming girls with the essential skills needed to achieve financial independence. Julina's approach of using age-appropriate tips and strategies interwoven with personal stories makes this the perfect guide to empower girls to handle their finances with confidence. As the mother of two girls myself, I feel this book is an essential tool for all parents of girls."

—Pam Keough, President & Chief Executive Officer
at Make A Wish Foundation of Connecticut, Inc.

"*Money Confident Girls* is an invaluable financial resource for young women. The author is focused on educating girls from a young age on basic financial concepts which are the foundation to a financially sound future. Julina Ogilvie draws in her audience with simple, yet powerful financial tools, strategies and habits demystifying the world of finance. The book removes the invisible barriers that have prevented women from confidently managing financial challenges. Education levels the playing field. Engaging women in developing their financial skills instills confidence. It empowers them to make effective decisions leading to financial independence. *Money Confident Girls* is a must read that every parent should share with their daughters."

—Susan Certoma, Board Director/Executive Leader/
Strategic Advisor

"Julina has started the important conversation and encourages all of us to continue it with the young girls in our families, lives, networks, etc. Whether you are a parent or not, helping the next generation of girls become confident and knowledgeable about their financial well-being will help all of us! Julina has outlined practical ideas and techniques to engage in the process of helping girls become more financially confident in a deeply personal (and humorous) way!"

—Julie L. Genjac, Vice President and Managing Director, Applied Insights, Hartford Funds

"Julina tackles the important topic of teaching girls about finances in her new book *Money Confident Girls*. This empowering guide is not only valuable for young girls but also for women of all ages. Julina dives deep into the challenges unique to women when it comes to managing their money. She addresses various concepts such as spending wisely, saving effectively, and building financial awareness. This book provides practical advice and actionable strategies that allow girls to approach their personal finances with confidence and clarity. By teaching girls early on about the value of money and how to make wise financial decisions, Julina instills in them a strong foundation for a prosperous future. Julina's passion for empowering girls shines through in every page, making this book a valuable resource for girls who aspire to take control of their financial futures. I wholeheartedly recommend *Money Confident Girls* to anyone who wants to empower the young girls in their lives and inspire them towards financial success."

—Courtenay Cooper Hall, Founder of BELLA Magazine

"My daughter recently posed an endearing and amusing question about whether her future husband should consider signing a prenuptial agreement. What touched me most was her recognition of the value we, as parents, have instilled in her life—a value she believes is worth protecting. *Money Confident Girls* is a powerful tool that equips parents to convey to their children that true wealth lies in mastering the art of financial knowledge, critical thinking, and proactive money management, whether they're just starting out at 10, navigating their twenties, or well into their fifties."

—Kay Cioffi, Chief Operating Officer,
JKSA RE Holdings, LLC

For permission requests, write to the publisher, addressed "Attention: Permissions Coordinator," at the address below.

Publish Your Purpose
141 Weston Street, #155
Hartford, CT, 06141

PYP **Publish**
Your Purpose

The opinions expressed by the Author are not necessarily those held by Publish Your Purpose.

Ordering Information: Quantity sales and special discounts are available on quantity purchases by corporations, associations, and others. For details, contact the publisher at hello@publishyourpurpose.com.

Edited by: Jill Kramek, Lily Capstick, August Li
Cover design by: Rebecca Pollock
Typeset by: Jet Launch

ISBN: 979-8-88797-081-3 (hardcover)
ISBN: 979-8-88797-082-0 (paperback)
ISBN: 979-8-88797-083-7 (ebook)

Library of Congress Control Number: 2023916073

First edition, January 2024.

Publish Your Purpose is a hybrid publisher of non-fiction books. Our mission is to elevate the voices often excluded from traditional publishing. We intentionally seek out authors and storytellers with diverse backgrounds, life experiences, and unique perspectives to publish books that will make an impact in the world. Do you have a book idea you would like us to consider publishing? Please visit PublishYourPurpose.com for more information.

Dedication

To my dearest Kaylin and Sidney,
From the very beginning, my greatest wish for you both has been to see you grow up as strong and healthy individuals, not only physically but mentally too. May you always believe in yourselves, embrace life's lessons with an open heart, and let your curiosity and thirst for knowledge lead you to infinite possibilities.

More than anything, I hope to impart upon you the invaluable gift of financial knowledge. Money is a tool that, when used wisely, can provide freedom, security, and opportunities to pursue your dreams. I wish for you to understand the value of hard work, saving, and investing, as well as the importance of giving back. May this knowledge empower you to navigate life's financial landscape with confidence and grace, enabling you to make sound decisions that align with your goals and aspirations.

With all my love and endless hope for your future,

Table of Contents

Preface

My career in finance has allowed me to engage in financial conversations with thousands of individuals. My responsibility was to discuss the markets, economy, and how our mutual funds might fit into their client's investments. This role included presentations and speaking engagements with their clients and prospects. From this, I observed behavior from the attendees that became eerily consistent.

The men were usually the ones who wanted to chat with me following a presentation. Most were confident about investing and were engaged with what was happening in the markets. Most women, on the other hand, when they did approach, were hesitant, admitting that they did not understand the markets or could not spend time on them. I commonly heard "Oh, I just let my husband handle it," or "I don't know much about investing." Many would also tell me about their apprehension toward investing. "I don't like risk," or "I'd rather put it in the bank." As crazy as this may sound, this was a consistent pattern from one event to the next.

Studies today prove there is a difference between how men and women think about money and investing. According to a Fidelity survey, only one-third of women see themselves as investors. Women are confident with being the CFO of the household and managing day-to-day finances, yet are less secure in long-term planning and investing (Fidelity Investments 2021).

How often do you attend a social event or stand at the side of a soccer field and hear women discuss finances? If you do, it is generally around finding a sale for a household item or their kids. Men? I am confident that you hear it more often. They will discuss the financial markets anywhere. You may hear, "Wow, did you see that the stock market fell today?" or "We made money in X investment." Why is it that finance today, for most women, appears to be a taboo topic, much like mental illness or addiction?

We all have experiences that shape our values and emotions, especially at an early age. These experiences shape how we think of and manage money. I have often heard from adults that they inherited their parent's frugalness; I certainly did. I am constantly turning off the lights when my family walks out of a room, reusing Ziploc bags, or pushing the envelope with our leftovers.

It is essential to acknowledge this early with children. In my life, I learned there were critical influences forming my beliefs and emotions at an early age. It began with my upbringing in South America. We spent the first six years of my life in São Paulo, Brazil, followed by several more years in Caracas, Venezuela. There was a lot about this upbringing that was not normal by American standards, such as hiding in bathtubs and fleeing cities that were under militia attack.

I have one memory of traveling with two other families by car into the depths of northern Brazil to camp for two weeks. As my parents tell it, after driving for twenty hours, we reached the borders of Brazil, Venezuela, and Guyana. We carried our food, water, tents, and generators for ten days.

We visited a tiny, impoverished village with mud-thatched homes during this trip. I recall children my age approaching me with virtually no clothes on. Although I spoke fluent Portuguese as a child, I do not remember speaking with them. I only recall that we were incredibly uncomfortable and intimidated by each other. Their curiosity seemed focused on my Velcro shoes, all the rage at the time for a kid. The looks on their faces as I showed them how to open and close these strips is a memory I have not forgotten. These families had nothing. No running water, no shoes—they barely had clothes and a place to sleep at night. To think of how you could live if you lost everything was a frightening experience for me. I attribute this experience to my emotions around money, and the anxiety and stress that I sometimes have after spending it. A worry that it will all just disappear one day.

My parents' divorce also taught me how money impacts a family. Before their separation, my father was unemployed, and they were open about the financial stress. Preparing to send me, their oldest child, off to college was undoubtedly part of the conversation. I felt guilty realizing what impact this had on them. I was suddenly old enough to comprehend the dynamics and emotions around money.

One night with my mother, I was filling out college applications, and the topic of income came up. Her comment then was, "Well, you should earn more money than your husband in case you ever divorce him." It was a startling response, but it was not surprising to me. I was old enough to know that my parents had marital issues, and within a year, they separated. Needless to say, that message stuck. With a divorce rate in the United States that seems to loom around 50%, it is hard not to acknowledge that women need financial independence, which should not begin after a divorce.

I did not realize it then, but I also began to stress about money. I had worked four different types of jobs by the time I finished high school. I babysat most weekends, coached the gymnastics pre-team, waitressed at a local Italian restaurant, and worked at my mother's real estate office. As embarrassing as it was for a teenage girl, I even dressed as a clown for my mother's office at the town fair to earn some cash.

My financial stress continued in college, and I constantly looked for ways to earn money. Some jobs were typical. I became the head steward for my sorority, where I cleaned dishes almost daily. I babysat for some athletic coaches, not earning very much. One family paid me five dollars an hour for five kids.

Other jobs were not so routine. I quickly observed that I could receive money back by collecting beer cans. Fraternity dumpsters on a Saturday or Sunday were the most lucrative, and I even convinced a friend to join me.

I dabbled in a jewelry business called Crystal Splendor. The idea was to make the jewelry from home (or in my dorm room). Selling the jewelry proved unsuccessful as they didn't like my finished product. I lost money with this business but created many laughs for my roommates.

I should have realized at this point that I was fixated on money, and it was not as if I had a poor upbringing. Yet the idea of not working and earning an income made me insecure and filled me with anxiety. I felt a constant need to have a job and an income stream. Two questions constantly gnawed at me: "Is it enough?" and "Is it sustainable?"

One positive outcome of all of these emotions was my determination to purchase my first condo in New Jersey soon after graduating from college. My mother and I surveyed many apartments in Jersey City, where my employer at the time, Lord, Abbett & Co., had recently relocated. I purchased a condo in one of the most ethnically diverse areas of the city and couldn't believe it when I sold it for a nice profit years later.

Upon graduating, finance seemed like the logical option. Additionally, two women solidified this path for me: my mother, Linda, and my grandmother, Ruth .

My mother has always been independent. She met my father, Bob, while studying at William & Mary, married him, and spent most of her marriage living together as expats, first in Thailand during the Vietnam War, followed by South America later with her three children. Linda taught at American schools and continued when we returned to the United States. After several years, she decided to pursue real estate.

Linda knew the potential to make more money in this career, and I can recall how hard she worked during this transition while managing school and sports for three children. Eventually, she became a top producer for Weichert Realtors, a large and prominent agency in northern New Jersey. She had one of the first car phones, this big clunky phone prominently displayed in the middle console of the car.

When my parents finally divorced, my mother continued her career and lived her life. A sign of her success was my brother, sister, and I would, on occasion, join her on her awards trips. To me, she represented the need to be independent, especially after a divorce.

The other person who solidified my path to a financial career was my grandmother, who, as I learned early on, was an incredibly independent woman. One of the first women to graduate from the University of Illinois, she created a nonprofit program in Asheville known as the Health Adventure, where kids learned about health and their bodies. The program was so successful that European countries studied and copied its blueprint.

One afternoon I joined my grandmother in cleaning out her and my grandfather's office. I noticed a metal box on her desk containing traditional index cards. When I asked her the purpose of the box, her response was, "Oh that... that is to prepare me if ever your grandfather passed away." This memory would be one of my first lessons in investing.

The first thing I learned about investing was that it meant one could own different types of assets. For my grandparents, this box organized what they owned. They didn't just have money in a bank, but owned different companies and real estate. Even a crematory! Another lesson my grandmother shared with me was the chance that she might outlive my grandfather, and she needed to be prepared. She was right. She outlived him by about ten years before she passed herself in 2020.

Incredibly, these discussions with my grandmother and mother are at the core of financial planning. Even decades later, my mother and grandmother defined the importance of having a financial plan. Women must be financially independent in case they have a divorce or outlive a spouse.

Today, as a mother of two young girls, it is not difficult for me to realize that financial literacy needs to start at a young age. This education is especially critical for young girls. In 2019 I created a podcast, *Women on Wealth*, to educate women on financial topics. One of my first interviews was with Patrina Dixon, a certified coach, international speaker, author, blogger, and podcaster. She is an advocate of financial literacy and helps individuals of all ages. When I asked her why she does what she does, her response was, "When you make an observation, you have an obligation." Her book series, *It'$ My Money*, has multiple volumes, all intended for teenagers between the ages of 13 and 18. But, she admits that, just as importantly, adults do not know many of the basics that she teaches.

Like most, the COVID-19 pandemic changed our family dynamic. My husband, Doug, who is also in finance, was home a lot more. I observed my discussions with Doug and my daughters about money, in particular about allowance. I realized that if two individuals who work in finance struggle with these conversations, I have an obligation to share with others the ideas and stories about finance that have been shared with me. This has led me to write this book.

Part 1

Building Money Confidence

1
Challenges Unique to Women

Confident girls aren't born, they're made.
—Unknown

Why do women struggle more with financial literacy than men? There is not one answer to this question. Women encounter several challenges that start at a very young age and remain throughout their entire lives.

SOCIAL INFLUENCES

These challenges often stem from social influences, which begin to shape the beliefs and values of young girls immediately. These influences are ever-present in the physical environment, the community, and the people that surround them. I can't help but look back to the 1950s as a reminder of what was expected of women during those times. Supposedly in 1955, a magazine article was published in *Housekeeping Monthly*, "The Good Wife's Guide." Although the validity of this article has been questioned, it does serve as a reference to how the role of a wife has changed. Some comments included:

> *"Have dinner ready.… Greet him with a warm smile and show sincerity in your desire to please him."*

> *"Catering to his comfort will provide you with immense personal satisfaction."*

> *"Listen to him.… Remember, his topics of conversation are more important than yours."*

We have come a long way since this was released. Women today have a more balanced role in family life, and many women are even primary breadwinners. Yet we still have a long way to go to remedy gender roles within our society and improve the underlying messages that we send our children. For example, social media continues to influence young girls negatively to this day. It can undermine their self-esteem and body image, thus increasing their anxiety and decreasing their confidence.

Gender-based marketing targets even the youngest generation with messaging on gender expectations. This remains prominent and influences how our girls think and act. Have you ever looked in a pharmacy at Band-Aid options? For girls there are all the Disney princesses, *Dora the Explorer,* and *Hello Kitty,* and for the boys *Star Wars* and the *Avenger Warriors.* Admittedly, I picked up these Band-Aids without a second thought around the messaging. This type of marketing across our society feeds into stereotypes that remain very different today for girls than boys.

THE GOOD GIRL

Does society today still influence the career that women choose? Dr. Patty Ann Tublin is an author, CEO, and founder of Relationship Toolbox LLC. "One of the reasons why women don't get paid what they're worth is because society, even in today's environment, has labeled certain jobs such as teaching, social work, and health care, as women's professions. Versus ones that we think of as male-oriented, such as engineering, investment banking, technology, and computer science."

This is because society has deemed women to have the role of being the good girl. As Tublin explains, "The good girl is the helper. The good girl wants to bring people together. Heaven forbid, the good girl wants to make money, like what is wrong with her? Nobody looks at a businessman and thinks he shouldn't make money."

When a woman wants to make money, the unconscious perception is that she's greedy, so she doesn't deserve it. "Even today, those unconscious biases exist in the corporate world. I see it, and I coach executive women. I have women who are incredibly successful, incredibly smart, on the A team with an Iivy Lleague education, and I have to help them strategize on how to ask for a raise. Women are not good at negotiating for themselves, but they're great at negotiating for others, especially their children (Tublin 2021).

Girls continue to receive messaging from society about how they should think and what roles they should play. If only we could expose them to positive encouragement and shield them from negative biases.

EDUCATION

The debate about what should be taught in schools is ongoing, and finance is part of this discussion. We've seen education shift over the decades. I recall my home economics class, where I learned how to boil water. It seems so silly looking back to think that I needed a lesson in how to do this, yet I don't recall being the only one who was clueless. According to the class description, budgeting and economics were part of this curriculum. My school must have missed this part, or it was such a small subset that it never resonated with me. I don't recall any financial lessons in school, and most individuals I ask will concur.

I brought this up in a women's group conversation as I was preparing to write this book, and they were all eager to share their experience. One woman shared her experience growing up in Connecticut in the 1980s with me. She told me about how in middle school she was taught how to be a "gracious and lovely host" and sew for her future husband. Even more incredulous were the lessons she shared with me on preparing snacks and appetizers for "unexpected guests" and combining mayonnaise and mustard as a dip.

Another woman shared with me how she had to take home economics classes while the boys took shop. I was personally allowed to choose one over the other and recall taking shop, which was woodworking. Now I believe there has been some progress since then. I even made a shelf I was proud to use in my bedroom, although I think it fell apart within a year.

A third woman I spoke with explained how her child signed up for what many parents and students at the time called a "throwaway" course—Math Basics. Her child had met all the requirements for the class and signed up without knowing what the course entailed. In her opinion, this class was one of the most important classes that her child ever took. It taught her child how to use a checkbook, the importance of a budget, and other basic financial concepts. Kudos to this school for offering such essential concepts to its students. What a shame that the value of this class was unknown to parents and students and described as a "throwaway" course.

Looking at what high school curriculums offer today, it's disappointing that only about half of the states offer a finance course that is not required. Even when states offer these courses, girls are less likely to take them than boys. These states that only offer a finance course, instead of requiring one, are likely doing a disservice to girls. Does this confidence gap affect the fields of study that girls choose? I'm sure the societal challenges we discussed also weigh in on these decisions. The areas of science, technology, engineering, and math (known as STEM) are all dominated by men. There have been initiatives to support STEM for girls, but we have a long way to go.

More likely than not, girls will choose other options rather than select economics or personal finance courses. Simon Platel is a retired managing director from an investment bank and has two girls, now in high school. They were with my girls one afternoon years ago and his oldest, Virginia, was describing high school to the other girls. As she was discussing her classes, I asked her which electives she had chosen. I was thrilled when she responded with finance and quickly followed up with, "My dad is making me take that course." With his professional background, her dad clearly understood the value of this selection. Despite having only chosen this course because of her dad's influence, she did later admit that she liked the course and found value in it.

Although there have been improvements, there remains a lot of frustration around finance in the education system. The research today is around education in high school. Any statistics found around middle and elementary school would be even more discouraging. The educational system by the state continues to disappoint parents and children as they become adults.

CONFIDENCE GAP

A loss of confidence is problematic for anyone, especially children. It can determine your career path and success, or rather lack of success. It can cause mental health issues such as stress, anxiety, and depression.

While there may be no significant difference in confidence between boys and girls in the early years, this dynamic changes quickly as girls age. The most significant change happens between the ages of eight and fourteen. By the time girls enter high school, they tend to hit their lows. They are more likely than boys to describe themselves as stressed, anxious, shy, emotional, and worried (Rox 2017).

As girls hit these lows, boys gain confidence. This is known as the *confidence gap*. There is speculation that this has worsened in the past decade with the influence of social media on girls. Teen girls are more likely than boys to face depression. That's not to say that boys don't ever lose confidence. They tend to lose it later.

I have seen this transition with my girls. Their initial confidence in the early days of attacking a sport, like skiing and gymnastics, was palpable. Over time, however, I have seen how this confidence slowly declines. What was once a mere fall off a beam or a stumble in a ski race evolves into something more intimidating, causing their once-strong confidence to wane.

Unfortunately, my youngest, Sidney, incurred knee injuries and a spine fracture during the COVID-19 pandemic. She spent several months away from the gym. Upon returning, her hesitancy shocked me. "Mom, it's getting more difficult and scarier," she often said. A year later, she had quit the sport. How could she lose so much confidence in such a short time? These experiences are not uncommon; I know they are not alone.

With low confidence comes stress, the pressure to be perfect, and the worry of failing. Almost half of the girls between twelve and thirteen believe that they are not allowed to fail. When asked what confidence means, most boys responded that it is "believing you can achieve anything." And what do girls say when asked the same question? "Being proud of who you are" (Y Pulse 2018). This is another example of the confidence gap.

Educating girls on financial literacy can be incredibly difficult, especially when they may be experiencing an emotional low. By the time girls reach their twenties, most of these skills and habits that pertain to finance are in place. Confidence is what creates action and reality from thoughts and wishes. As we build confidence and see success, it motivates us to continue acting with confidence. Even when we fail, this confidence is how we get back on our feet and try again.

WAGE GAP

We've been discussing the *wage gap* between men and women for decades, and it remains a problem. Women continue to earn less than men, roughly 82 cents for every dollar men earn. (Aragâo, 2023) While this has undoubtedly improved, it has been slow, and we still have a long way to go.

The cause for this gap isn't one factor but several. The first to consider is that women choose different career paths than men. In my career, in the finance industry, only a small percentage of women exist. The COVID-19 pandemic, for example, was dubbed the "Shecession." The industries hit the hardest were the leisure, hospitality, health care, and education, all of which had a disproportionate impact on women.

Another consideration is that women are much more likely to take a break during their careers to have children or become a caregiver to a parent. They will take lower-paid positions, turn down promotions, and take significant time off to accommodate their family. These decisions are justified, offering more flexibility to manage their family responsibilities, but there is a financial cost. When women decide to take a break from work, they need to consider the impact on the family of no longer having an income. Often, they can justify the decision to work less because the income they forgo is either less than or equal to the costs of daycare or nursing care required while at work. How many women have you come across, whether friends, family, or colleagues, that have shared their unique stories and decided to leave the workforce?

A lack of confidence in the workforce is another consideration that Dr. Patty Ann Tublin addresses. "We're all working for money, as we should, and that's not something women should shy away from. But because women are known for having difficulty negotiating, companies will more likely pay them less because there won't be pushback. So, the gender wage gap, believe it or not, starts immediately out of school. They've done the research and asked young men and women how much money they expect to make starting out when they first get out of school. Women say that they expect to make approximately $5000 less as a starting salary than men. And that gap just continues to grow throughout their career."

As problematic as the wage gap is during a woman's working career, the gap magnifies into their retirement years. Women often have fewer savings in their retirement accounts. In 2019, the Vanguard Group published a paper and found that men, on average, have 51% more than women in their account balance. This variance is due to the higher wages men receive, making it easier for them to maximize their plan contributions. If a retirement plan also offers employer contributions that match a percentage of their income, this only enhances the savings difference between men and women (Vanguard Research 2019). With fewer savings, they will have to find other means of income and spend less, all with more stress.

Women will also retire with less Social Security due to the wage gap. Whether a woman leaves the workforce for some time or even chooses not to leave the workforce, studies show that the earnings record of women with the same number of years working as men will receive lower Social Security benefits. Women receive, on average, 80% of the benefits that men receive (Edna and Gale 2020). Retirement savings and Social Security are at the core of a solid retirement plan. With lower amounts in each, coupled with living longer (which we'll discuss later on), this presents a significant challenge for women in retirement.

DIVORCE

The divorce rate today is unsettling and disproportionately affects women negatively. In the United States, it currently sits at around 50%. Following a divorce, fewer women will remarry than men (Montenegro 2015). This is problematic for women because, during their marriage, many are unaware of the family finances and investments. I repeatedly hear this from women who struggled to manage their finances and investments following a divorce. In some cases, their spouse moved or hid money from them, creating more of a struggle after their separation.

In one study of women who divorced or separated after the age of fifty, women's household income fell by almost twice as much as men's (United States Government Accountability Office 2017). The primary cause of this statistical difference, as we previously discussed, is that women more frequently choose to leave the workforce and become the primary caregiver for their children within a marriage.

It is also common, following a divorce, for the woman to maintain full custody of the children. Full custody becomes incredibly challenging for women, especially if they are without paid work or working part-time and relying on alimony that the court deemed "appropriate" (if they are lucky to receive it at all). With limited resources, women will only focus on the short-term and their children. What they will lack from this is long-term financial preparation, such as planning for retirement and ensuring they do not become a burden for their children in the future.

An example of such a divorce comes from a business owner who recently retired successfully and moved to Spain. He shared his mom's struggles following his parents' divorce when he was six. His father was wealthy, and his mother was not. He would volley back and forth between his father's mansion and his mother's apartment. He recalls the clothes his dad bought for him, which could only be worn at his house. He couldn't take them to school or his mother's apartment. She had to purchase different clothes for him on her own. His grandmother stepped in to pay for a tennis club for him to attend. He described his mindset: "I always felt like an intruder. Money was held against me."

His mother found herself in the unfortunate situation that many women face after a divorce. She faced financial struggles, and these difficulties had a cascading impact on her son. Unfortunately, in this situation, his father only exacerbated the situation leaving an even more fractured family.

LONGEVITY GAP

More and more people are reaching the age of one hundred than ever before. Women also continue to outlive men by about two to four years on average—this is known as the *longevity gap* (Health-View Services 2023). Although this should be a good thing, it is problematic when it comes to women's finances.

Today, one common concern I hear is, "I'm scared of running out of money." This comment is justified, especially with rising health care costs. Health care has quadrupled over the past 50 years, all while the cost of other goods and services has either grown at a more moderate rate or even decreased. In 1958, per capita health expenditures were $134, including care paid for by government or private health insurers. By 2012, this per capita health spending soared to $8,953 (Conover 2012). This rising cost represents inflation, characterized by a rise in prices that results in a decline in purchasing power over time. In other words, the value of a dollar today diminishes as time progresses. While this is applicable to all goods and services, it holds even greater significance concerning health care costs.

Two to four years of outliving men may not seem like a big difference, yet for a healthy couple in their mid-forties today, women are expected to pay about $200,000 more in healthcare costs during retirement than men (HealthView Services 2023). The idea of running out of money is terrifying, and it is no wonder that it creates so much anxiety.

Given the longevity gap and the high divorce rate, there's an important statistic that women need to consider: 90%. Meaning, 90% of women will find themselves managing their finances at some point (Harrison and McCormick 2019). Most women will not be prepared for this event, and following a divorce or the death of a spouse is certainly not the time to "wake up" and try and get a handle on their finances.

DEBT

Debt continues to be one of the most challenging issues we face today. It continues to rise to new all-time highs. As if household and credit card debt isn't enough, the fastest-growing level of debt today is student loan debt. More and more students are graduating from four-year public and private colleges with higher debt levels than ever. Can you guess who holds the majority of this debt? Women. According to the Education Data Initiative, 58% of all student loan debt belongs to women, and it takes an average of two years longer for them to pay off this debt (Hanson, 2023).

I recall reviewing my loan options in high school while preparing for college. It was overwhelming. Questions like when to apply, how to apply, and how to pay it off were all on my mind. So many students in debt today are not in this situation due to a lack of preparation. I always see families working hard to put money away for their children's education. So many will say to me that it just seems like it is never enough. The cost is too high!

There are, of course, long-term effects of this debt. Recent data shows that many young adults have no retirement savings before their thirties. Even adults in their forties have limited savings, which becomes particularly challenging as they decide whether to have children and face the considerable expenses that come with it (Federal Reserve 2019). Where there is debt, there are typically limited savings for the future.

2
Build Independence

*Freedom is never more than one generation away
from extinction. We didn't pass it to our children in the
bloodstream. It must be fought for, protected,
and handed on for them to do the same.*

—Ronald Reagan

SUPER BUBBLE

Parents want to shelter and protect kids from everything. Hence the term "helicopter parents," which refers to parents who are overprotective and overly involved in their children's school, activities, and even relationships. Kids aren't allowed to make mistakes. Millennials today describe this as growing up in a "super bubble." While the intention is good, the outcome can be disastrous.

This is no different when it comes to finance. We don't want these girls making poor money decisions, just like we don't want them to make mistakes. However, if there is ever a time to allow girls to learn from their mistakes, it's early on. It's better to make mistakes with small amounts of money than later in life with larger financial decisions. Choosing the wrong $20 toy can create a sense of regret for a girl, forcing her to start all over again with their savings. This mistake can be just as impactful as purchasing the wrong $20,000 car or $200,000 condo.

Or maybe instead of making an incorrect purchase, they lose their money. I recall the look of agony when my oldest, Kaylin, realized that money had been taken from her room. We recently had some work done on our house, and we can only assume that one of the workers took $20 from her savings jar. One of the early reality checks is that life isn't fair and sometimes something you have earned can be taken from you, even from what you would consider a safe place. She no longer saves her money in an open jar on her shelf. Despite her disappointment, this was a lesson in managing her finances and not an experience that she will forget.

This is a slippery slope for many; I'm shocked as to how many individuals today feel compelled to financially rescue their child or even grandchild. One family I know continues to financially support their son, who is in his forties, married with children, yet he relies on his parents to pay for large items such as a car and a home. Has he learned from this? I don't think so; after being employed for about 20 years, he still has no savings. He doesn't have that sense of independence and unfortunately, it doesn't appear he ever will.

BATH AND BODY WORKS

As these girls build independence, they will also experience success. When my youngest, Sidney was nine, I brought her to Bath and Body Works for the first time. For anyone that's never shopped in that store, they always have bundle deals like "buy three for X" or "get these five for Y." For girls learning about allowance and how to spend money, it's definitely worth the time. Admittedly, that was not my original purpose for visiting the store.

After my daughter sorted out her purchase and we stood in line, she asked me to stand behind her. She wanted to check out on her own; how could I say no? I hesitated as a line started to form behind us but did as she asked. She walked to the counter by herself—that act alone made me so proud! She handed everything over and when the polite woman told her the amount, she proceeded to go into her wallet to pull the money out. She successfully handed the money to the woman, yet when she accepted the change, she managed to spill the coins all over the counter and floor. I rushed to help but she held me back and said, "Mom, I can handle it." I don't know if it's because I stepped back and allowed her the independence she wanted or if they were genuinely patient, but the line that had formed did not press on. This experience turned into a genuine lesson, although unintended, and the outcome could not have been better planned. The pride on her face is something a parent cannot forget.

POWDERED MILK

Judi Otton, Founder of GrowthCast, shared with me the source of her independence and success. Raised by her mom after her parents divorced when she was nine, she recalled their financial struggles and their reliance on government assistance. One lasting memory from that difficult time was not having enough money for real milk and living off powdered milk. By the time she was ten, she had decided that she was going to "get a good job so I can marry whoever I want. Not for money."

She did just that. She went on to get an engineering degree in college, now owning her own firm. She jokes that she makes more money than her husband. This is another example that not all of our memories are positive; however, even the negative ones can turn it into something positive.

The influence of mothers during this time can be incredibly powerful. Studies show that during the elementary school years, girls want to follow the career path of their mother more than their father. Girls need to learn from their failures; it's best to do so when the consequences are minor. They must be accountable for their actions and the resulting outcomes. If they don't take ownership of their mistakes and are always rescued by their parents, how will they take their finances seriously? As difficult as it may be, we need to let them fall from time to time and fight the urge to help them get up. Of course, this is easier said than done.

3

What Is Financial Literacy?

*The number one problem in today's generation and
economy is the lack of financial literacy.*

—Alan Greenspan

What is financial literacy? If this is a question that you're not quite sure how to answer, you are not alone. The simple answer is that it's the knowledge and application of financial skills. As simple as it may seem, a considerable number of adults, particularly women, struggle to understand and manage their finances in this fashion. There are five key components to financial literacy known as "My Money Five" (Financial Literacy and Education Commission 2023).

Earn: Make the most of what you earn by understanding your pay and benefits.

Spend: Be sure you are getting a good value, especially with big purchases, by shopping around and comparing prices and products.

Save and invest: It's never too early to start saving for future goals such as a house or retirement, even by saving small amounts.

Borrow: Borrowing money can enable essential purchases and build credit, but interest costs can be expensive. And, if you borrow too much, you will have a large debt to be repaid.

Protect: Take precautions about your financial situation, accumulate emergency savings, and have the right insurance.

As we age and our finances become more important, so does the complexity of financial literacy. It's like children learning math in school. A student in high school can't complete calculus without learning algebra in middle school, which isn't possible without understanding the fundamentals of addition, subtraction, multiplication, and division in elementary school. The concepts we teach our children in financial literature fall similarly. The longer we wait to introduce these concepts, the more difficult it becomes to understand and benefit from the knowledge. For this reason, financial education must start at a young age.

During the formative years—starting from when our girls are mere toddlers through elementary school—the focus is on instilling good money habits and a positive money mindset. Building the fundamentals around earning, spending, saving, sharing, and giving is also essential. Learning how to allocate among these areas is also important as it sets the foundation for budgeting.

These fundamentals will continue to evolve into more substantial concepts with significant implications for their financial future as they enter their teenage years. The importance of earnings and finding the right job for many begins at this age. Some important concepts for them will be:

- Understanding and adhering to a budget.
- Recognizing the importance of savings.
- Grasping the matter of compound interest.
- Comprehending how rates of return impact savings.
- Receiving an introduction to investing with cash, stocks, and bonds.

They will need to learn how to write a check, build credit, look at financial aid opportunities, and understand ways to start investing for their future. All of these are critical during the teenage years, but no child can get there without the lessons of the formative years.

Finally, as they become adults and begin to look at creating careers, they must understand the benefits and retirement plans that come with these opportunities. Additionally, they'll need to learn how to purchase a first apartment or home, merge finances with a partner or spouse, and create an estate plan. Again, none of this is possible without the building blocks taught over the years.

The importance of financial literacy is certainly not new, yet it remains a challenge for most people today, both in the United States and worldwide. One global study defines financial literacy as an individual that can correctly explain three out of four fundamental concepts: risk diversification, inflation, numeracy (interest), and compound interest. At the country level, financial literacy rates vary significantly, ranging from 71% to only 13%. The good news is that the US is not at 13%, that would be Yemen. The bad news is that neither are we the 71%, that would be Norway. In fact, the US came in at 57%, behind the United Kingdom, Switzerland, and Sweden (Klapper et al. 2015).

Not only is financial literacy a global challenge, it disproportionately affects women compared to men. One survey comments,
"Not only are female respondents less likely to answer financial
literacy questions correctly but they are also more likely to state
that they do not know the answers to the questions. The gender
gap in financial literacy continues to persist even after taking into
account marital status, education, income, and other socioeconomic
characteristics" (Bucher-Koenen et al. 2014). Financially literate
individuals can make more informed decisions regarding financial
topics and increase their ability to live the way they choose. There
is an increased amount of data showing strong links between financial literacy and mental health. It makes sense when you consider
that financial literacy can increase economic security, resulting in less
anxiety, stress, and depression. According to the Money and Mental
Health Policy Institute, poor finances often lead to stress and anxiety
that can further impact finances. People with debt also have a mental
health diagnosis in 46% of the cases.

4

Money Mindset

Money doesn't have beliefs about you.
You have beliefs about money.

—Joe Vitale

Another vital variable in this discussion, especially concerning young girls, is the concept of *money mindset*. Money mindset pertains to your individual beliefs and attitudes toward money. How you think about money will influence how you drive your decisions around your finances.

Raechelle Minney is the founder of Financial Fitness Unleashed, which focuses on financial wellness for women. Similar to my career, she experienced how emotional we are regarding our finances, particularly women. As Raechelle Minney describes, "There are things happening in our mind so quickly, and most likely, we're drawing upon past experiences that have led us to a certain belief, and then we decide. Before you know it, it's a very cyclical process, but it happens so fast in our mind, the decision is made. And then we have these feelings. And what's so interesting is because it's happening so fast, I don't think many of us ever stopped in the middle of that decision-making framework, to hit the pause button on life. And say, I wonder why I'm reacting so strongly to this decision, or I've had such an emotional tie to that outcome" (Minney 2022).

These young girls are like sponges, absorbing your actions and behaviors, which will eventually shape their money mindset over time. Think of all the comments you yourself heard about money growing up. Some common phrases that kids will hear include:

- "Money doesn't grow on trees."
- "Let's save it for a rainy day."
- "There's not enough money to go around."
- "We're going to the poorhouse."
- "Do you think we live in a barn?"
- "We can't afford it."
- "That's a waste of money."

Will these children, as they get older, internalize and embrace these ideas, or reject them? I grew up hearing, "Do you think we live in a barn?" I've become obsessed with this because I find myself saying the same thing to my girls. I constantly walk around the house, turning off the lights. "Do you know how much it costs to keep the lights on all day?" For the most part they ignore me, as I did at their age. I wonder how they will act as adults. Will they too become a bit obsessive about turning the lights off?

These phrases can certainly be influential; think of some other factors that may influence your money memories.

- What's your earliest memory of money?

- How were your parents with money? Did they have fears of money or did they spend it however they pleased?
- What did you learn from your parents about money? Was it from observations or conversations?
- Did you receive an allowance growing up? If so, how were you paid?
- How old were you when you first earned money? How did you feel?
- What guidance did you receive when you received money?
- Was there any emotional trauma around money? Was there fear around money?

To discuss money, have a plan on how to answer broad questions that will come up. Don't brush off your children. If they ask questions about money, give an honest answer that's age-appropriate.

- How much money do you make?
- Are we rich or poor?
- Why is our house not as big as _____?
- Why can't you just buy me this toy with your card?

As I have shared, I recall several experiences and conversations that formed the money mindset that I have today. Very often with money memories, one of two things will occur: Either we internalize these memories and turn them into beliefs of our own, as I do by running around my house turning off all of the lights just as my parents did. Or we take these same memories and form beliefs in the opposite direction. For instance, in discussing money mindset with a speaker on my podcast, she shared with us how she grew up in a house where her parents refused to put the air conditioner on and she was constantly hot. Today in her own home, she's proud that she can turn the air conditioner on throughout the summer and her parents complain how cold it is when they come to visit.

Very often, negative memories have an impact on children that create positive money mindsets. One of the most impactful stories I have heard comes from Lyly Ha. Lyly is the head of product innovation at a professional service firm in New York City. In an interview with her, she began, "I am a survivor. I experienced many dramatic events starting when I was very young and lost everything, including my home, in a socialist takeover. There were lots and lots of emotional and financial hardships. And it took me a while to finally recover and be able to talk about it."

Lyly was born in Saigon, Vietnam, into a very wealthy family. After the fall of Saigon, with tanks rolling down her street, her family lost everything. "We had multiple homes, money in the bank, and assets. Everything was frozen as if we were criminals, and the comfortable life we had disappeared overnight. We had to start everything from scratch. The ruling party tried to control the currency by exchanging money four times during my nine years under their rule. It was like I got to play the Monopoly game in a real-life situation where everyone became equal at "go" four different times. Then it quickly became unequal. When inequality happened, every household started again with the same amount. That was my childhood."

When Lyly was ten, her dad was in a wheelchair, and her mom, a pharmacist, was forced to find an hourly labor job making shoes to support the family. Lyly and her sister received a daily budget to buy food at the market, so they bargained for everything. "At ten years old, I had to calculate what I could purchase for the day and negotiate it to the penny, and if I didn't do it well, there was not enough food for my family. So I had a lot of emotions growing up, and I think they are both good and bad. On the positive side, the experience has taught me to be super resilient, persistent, and continue learning to overcome obstacles and challenges. Anything that's come to me I've had to overcome." On the flip side, her money mindset is one of discomfort, "I have done well in the US and love this country, but I'm always afraid everything will be gone." Lyly finally came to the United States at eighteen years old with $500 provided by her sister, who was already here. She spoke no English, took a loan, and was able to graduate from college and achieve a great professional career.

A more positive money memory is explained by Raechelle Minney. Her most impactful money memory revolves around her father, an entrepreneur in real estate. She shares that her father would constantly talk to her about money. She loved these discussions, which centered around how to earn money and why it's important, and even involved bringing her to look at real estate. Part of this interest, she admits, was just the joy of spending time with him. Reflecting back, she comments, "Wow, how unique is that experience compared to a lot of other people's experience with money. I'm super grateful that he instilled that in me so early."

The money memories these girls experience will come in all sizes and have positive and negative effects. They will build their money mindset over time, but be mindful that they are watching and observing yours! Acknowledging this fact is an essential first step toward creating a more positive money mindset. Ultimately, this approach helps in nurturing a Money Confident Girl who is strong and independent in her own way.

5

Habits

Habits are the compound interest of self-improvement. The same way that money multiplies through compound interest, the effects of your habits multiply as you repeat them.

—James Clear

Positive habits are essential. Today, there is a lucrative industry full of self-help books, coaches, and even apps to help us create habits. This extends to various aspects of our lives, from managing our physical activity, eating habits, and consumption of substances like smoking and drinking, to how we manage our finances.

I read *Atomic Habits* by James Clear, a book that emphasizes how making small changes can result in remarkable results. As Clear explains, "The effects of your habits multiply as you repeat them. They seem to make little difference on any given day, yet the impact they deliver over the months and years can be enormous. It is only when looking back two, five, or perhaps ten years later that the value of good habits and the cost of bad ones becomes strikingly apparent."

Habits are easier to build in young girls than in adults. They are innocent, unaware of alternatives, and less likely to question. As they get older, these changes and habits become much more challenging to adopt.

Also, the longer we act on a habit, the easier it will stick. The same goes for negative habits—breaking them can be exceptionally challenging. If this is the case, we must create good habits early in our girls. Their habits form early, sooner than most expect. In children, they take root by the age of nine, but other studies suggest even earlier.

BALANCING A CHECKBOOK

One positive habit I acquired at a young age and have held onto is balancing a checkbook. In today's digital era, most individuals no longer balance a checkbook, with everything being managed online. Yet I still balance a checkbook, although rather than using a small checkbook, I use a simple, eight-inch journal notebook with lined paper. My husband makes fun of me for doing this. Yet it is my way of processing my spending. This monthly ritual of reviewing and balancing the notebook serves as my mental check.

My father taught me how to do this when I opened my first bank account. I recall the two of us sitting at the kitchen table in New Jersey, and him showing me how to write a check and then enter it into the checkbook. I can't imagine this habit of mine going away, ever.

Unfortunately, not everything we learn or the habits we develop are beneficial to us. Many can be detrimental to us. How do we foster good habits at a young age instead of creating bad habits? Some bad habits can evolve into a financial disaster. These are found in individuals of all ages. These bad habits include:

- Not paying attention to the price.
- Buying a large purchase frivolously.
- Not having a budget.
- Not having an emergency fund.
- Not planning for long-term goals.
- Not maximizing investment options.
- Not aligning investments with your goals.

THE CREWNECK

One bad habit I am working through with Sidney is not paying attention to the price. We don't often go to stores to purchase things, especially since the pandemic. Most of our purchases are on Amazon; she will see something she likes and save it to my cart. When she really wants something, she'll follow me around with my iPad until I complete the purchase. I have come to realize that she often has no idea of the cost associated with what she wants. One purchase was for a crewneck, and when I asked her how much it cost, her response was, "I don't know." I asked her to go in and tell me, and she realized that it was over $65 with $20 in shipping alone (even though we are Prime members).

As consumers, our shopping patterns continue to shift, which can alter our habits. Where once cash and checkbooks were the primary tools used to manage our finances, we now use credit cards and online purchases. These are all my girls are accustomed to. The benefit is the convenience of purchasing virtually any item we want at any time. As our girls embrace these methods, understanding how and where they spend their money becomes vital.

The danger of this convenience is not planning and prioritizing what we buy. Many adults struggle with their finances and spend their money as soon as it's available. This is evident by the high level of consumer debt in this country. Monitoring how these girls spend their money allows us to have open financial discussions. We can guide them through these purchasing decisions. When they inevitably make mistakes, we can offer our support to help them learn from these decisions and make better choices in the future.

SAMMY RABBIT

Sammy Rabbit is a character created almost 20 years ago to help anyone talk to kids about money. Through children's books, songs, and other resources, this character creates positive money habits for children, starting as young as the age of three. Sammy Rabbit Money School describes their mission as:

> Understanding how to acquire and manage money is vital to leading a successful, secure, and healthy life. Starting the process early is essential. The problem: kids' money habits and attitudes form much earlier than many people realize. In fact, Cambridge University research indicates that adult money habits are set by age 7! Studies reflect a lack of financial literacy has become a worldwide epidemic. The wrong financial habits debilitate kids' dreams and futures. The right financial habits empower them.

The founder of Sammy Rabbit Money School is Sam Renick. In an interview with him for my podcast, he primarily discussed how they were focused on habit formation. One of his core messages is: "saving is a great habit."

He further explained, "If you create this routine and this repetitive cycle, it's a proven time-tested recipe. It may not make you rich overnight, but it's very predictable. It's going to systematically advance your financial security, independence, wealth, and all of that stuff."

TEACHING MOMENTS

Financial instincts are not something that we are born with, and someone must spend the time to teach this to us, just like we teach our kids how to say please and thank you, cross the street, or use an oven. These teaching moments don't need to be a sit-down strategy session. They can be part of your day-to-day conversations, errands, visual activities, and games.

Creating good financial habits and avoiding bad ones need to be addressed early. Everyday events and conversations can evolve into teachable moments that build these girls' knowledge, habits, and confidence. This is not a quick process with immediate results, but small steps will create a remarkable impact over time. This allows the compound interest to evolve as described in *Atomic Habits*.

6

Money Is Finite

*Money doesn't grow on trees but
grows on intelligent minds.*

—Matshona Dhliwayo

Growing up, I heard "Money doesn't grow on trees" a lot, probably because I thought it did. I would stand in a store demanding my parents purchase one item or another, with no care as to where the money came from.

A GIRL'S CLOSET

One such memory comes from fifth grade, when I was still adjusting to life in the States and trying to acclimate to a new town. One new friend that I met had an unbelievable closet full of clothes and brands that I had never heard of. At the time, the brand Benetton was all the craze and new to me. I certainly wasn't aware of how much it cost. One night as my mom sat at the kitchen table, I proceeded to bring down the wardrobe from my closet and throw it onto the table, demanding a new wardrobe. I recall the look on her face, mortified that I would do this, especially in front of a friend. "How do you think we're going to pay for this?" I heard this a lot as well.

I can't imagine what it would have been like in today's world of scrolling through Amazon or the Lululemon website. A girl's closet today is the checkout cart on an app or website. This is what my girls do, and then they proceed to follow me around the house, wearing me down, as my impatience grows. And yes, sometimes it works, I hate to admit it. Money is finite, it's tangible. As simple as this might seem, it's the foundation of money. Every child will have a closet or checkout cart and will try the patience of their parents as they learn this concept.

VAIL RESORTS

Some of the largest corporations worldwide are aware of this trend. My family skis in Vermont at Okemo Mountain, which was acquired years ago by Vail Resorts. We now ski on their Epic Pass, which offers unlimited skiing at all of their global resorts for an annual fee. Another benefit is linking your credit card to your pass at their restaurants. On weekends in the ski lodge, it's hard not to notice the hundreds of kids in the ski program that come through for lunch, pull their ski passes out, and swipe to purchase their lunch. There's no need to consider the cost and pull the appropriate money out. Yes, it's convenient, but do our kids miss out on understanding the value of how much money they spend? I have asked my daughter on occasion how much money she would spend; initially, the response was a shrug, but now that I bug her, she has started to pay attention.

Children must learn that money is finite. There is no infinite supply at the other end of these cards they use. It can run out if not appropriately managed—this lesson will carry through life. At a young age, start with cash and coins. What's young? I once heard that it's appropriate to start teaching children about spending when they stop putting coins in their mouths. Start with the coins, they're easier to identify with their different sizes. As you show your children these coins, quiz them on the value of a penny, nickel, dime, and quarter. Which is more or less?

WHAT IS A CHECK?

Not only are kids today not carrying cash, but they are also not familiar with the use of checks. I stood at the kitchen counter one Saturday paying bills. Like most people today, we pay almost everything online. However, a bill from a landscaper came in the mail, so I proceeded to write them a check. I was signing the check when Sidney, at the time ten years old, asked me what I was doing. When I responded that I was paying one of our bills, she replied, "It doesn't look like it." She had never seen a check. Although adults today aren't using checks the way they might have in the past, there are still occasional uses for them. Therefore, it's important for kids to learn about how checks work and when to use them.

A CARDBOARD BOX

Many of our girls' family members tape money in their birthday cards. One grandmother takes it one step further. Instead of gifting a $10 bill, let's say, she includes the $10 in ten separate bills. As these dollars accumulate, the parents save it in a brown cardboard box with a handmade label on the side. Birthday money. Within the box, the dollars are neatly lined. This process is done so that the kids can see and learn the value of these bills. They want their children to understand this value and treat it accordingly.

PLAYING GROCERY

Another way to reinforce the value of money is by playing grocery. One such example shared with me by Matt Gudonis is the use of a small sandwich shop role-playing game. The shop includes fake ingredients to make sandwiches, such as meat, cheese, toppings, drinks, chips, and cookies. The child sets the price, and the family pays for the made-to-order sandwiches. In this example, the child has set the price of the sandwiches at $100 and goes heavy on the black olives and red onion toppings (hopefully a free mint is included!). The parents have been working toward a more reasonable amount, say $10, that more accurately reflects the real-world value of money for such items. At the age of four, preschool has taught them how to count, but they're still learning to add, identify different bills, and assign a value to money.

You can play a game with your girl when you're out at a store or restaurant. Give her a dollar amount to spend and the freedom to decide what to purchase. If you pay with cash, ask her to count. If you are owed money, ask her to calculate how much change you are due. In a restaurant, she can work on her percentages during the tipping process. There is tremendous value to be learned from this participation.

I have enjoyed taking my girls to a store, and then watching them pick out their purchases, line up at the cashier, and pay for the items by themselves. I have witnessed many patient retailers behind us, allowing them to walk through this process as they pull money out of their wallet and count it all on the counter. Many parents have experienced stress as their child holds up a line to do this. Whether we are in a rush or have a line of customers behind us, we instinctively want to handle the purchase ourselves and move on. But the counting process is an essential mental step for kids. The counting process is done best with actual dollars and coins in the real world, despite some frustration.

The experience of these girls will be ongoing and evolve as they build values around money. There are four financial fundamentals to build upon as a toddler that we will discuss: earning, spending, saving, and investing. These basic money concepts are the building blocks for their future.

Part 2

The Financial Foundation

7

Earning Is Empowering

An investment in knowledge pays the best interest.
—Benjamin Franklin

Often, as children begin to purchase items on their own, the discussion about how to earn money naturally emerges. There is tremendous value in a child who wants to earn money, as they will feel a sense of pride when they succeed. This provides them with an opportunity to explore options and build independence as they decide how they might want to earn money.

Some ways young girls earn money around the neighborhood include: washing cars, cleaning, mowing lawns, shoveling driveways, taking care of pets, or bringing in mail for a family that is away. You may decide to pay them for certain chores or projects in your own home such as walking the dog, doing laundry, weeding the garden, or vacuuming the house.

LEMONADE

For many girls, the first way they earn money is through a lemonade stand. My girls' first attempt at this was when they were about six and eight. They confidently made the lemonade and carted it down our long driveway in a wagon. It wasn't a paved driveway, so half of the lemonade spilled by the time they arrived. I also didn't dare tell them that "lemon aid" was spelled incorrectly. Nor did I tell them that location is key for a successful lemonade stand. Our road at the time was very private and windy. After hours of standing there, I believe they only sold one lemonade to our neighbor. She felt sorry for them and paid $5, so the girls still felt a sense of accomplishment.

They learned from this experience. Years later, the lemonade stand has seen improvements. They learned to spell lemonade, found a better location a block away from the public beach in town, and proudly noted on their sign that they accept Venmo, so no more excuses of not carrying cash. One afternoon, Sidney and a friend sat outside for hours and they sold not only lemonade but handmade jewelry that they had put together. It was a scorching day, and they each sat under personal umbrellas, grabbing the attention of anyone walking by. That afternoon they made well over $50.

As impressed as I was (and relieved to have something to keep them busy during the summer), there was competition all around them. Competition is a way for kids to build on their entrepreneurial skills by building their brand, marketing, and services. The stand that stood out was run by a group of kids who had a large six-foot-tall stand their parents helped position at one of the busiest blocks near the beach. They offered not only lemonade but baked goods as well. They were impressive; it was hard not to stop.

NEGOTIATING

When girls start to earn, they can learn to negotiate. I would prefer they fine-tune these skills at a young age with family rather than when they are older and off on their own in the professional world. It's actually quite entertaining. As I write this, Sidney tried to negotiate with my husband when she cooked us dinner one night. "You should pay me because you wouldn't eat if I didn't make this."

Young girls are clever. Mary Ellen, an executive director for a nonprofit, told me how her daughter learned to negotiate her allowance with her younger brother. She came home one day to find him standing on a chair at the kitchen sink, rinsing dishes to load into the dishwasher, a chore for which her daughter was paid an allowance. When asked why he was doing her job, he responded that his sister was paying him. She had arranged to give him half of her pay for doing her chores and was keeping the other half for herself.

SEARCHING FOR A FIRST JOB

Searching for a first job is a daunting step for children. Girls want to spend money as they wish and often welcome this opportunity. Giving them this independence allows them to learn the concept of a trade-off early on. They may want to spend all their money on one expensive clothing item, making most parents cringe. If they choose to do this, they may quickly realize how fast their earned money can go. If so, parents may need to guide them on these future decisions.

Typically, a child's first job will be in middle school. It will be local, centered around a sport, cause, or activity they love. The most common first jobs are babysitting, dog walking, or pet sitting. Some other jobs might include working at a local retail store, restaurant, or golf course.

I did all of the above, but mostly babysat. Babysitting is an excellent first job for responsible girls who love younger children and can take care of them. Typically, girls will start babysitting at around twelve or thirteen, especially if they have younger siblings and are already comfortable with the role.

It's recommended to take a babysitting course before becoming a babysitter. There are many local classes you can find. For example, our pediatrician's office sponsors several a year. One of the most notable babysitting courses is run by the Red Cross. Sometimes, the Red Cross will offer these courses at schools and community centers.

These classes are designed for girls who are between the ages of eleven and fifteen. They can take about six hours to complete. Babysitting courses can now even be taken online to provide more flexibility to students. The courses train students on safety, maintaining discipline, feeding, changing diapers, and first-aid procedures, including CPR and AED training. Some of the questions that these courses cover include: Should they call 911 instead of the child's parents for help? What if the child is not listening to them? What questions do they need to ask the parents about their child and the schedule for the night? There's even an entrepreneurial component where they learn about managing a business, professionalism, and expanding their business.

The popularity of these courses has grown over the decades. I don't recall ever taking one despite all of my babysitting jobs, including work with newborns. These courses are an excellent way for girls to stand out from other babysitters. The Red Cross claims that 80% of parents are willing to pay more for a babysitter with Red Cross babysitting credentials (American Red Cross 2023). When they've completed the course, they will receive an official certification with a unique ID or QR code, allowing potential employers to verify their course completion.

The job search process is another element. A referral from a family member or friend is a great first start, so make sure that your daughter shares her enthusiasm for this job opportunity with them. You can also encourage your daughter to advertise her services, another great skill to learn at a young age.

Social media is the most common way to advertise babysitting credentials. Parents or girls can post these job opportunities to connect them with their local community. The two most common social media platforms for babysitters I find are private Facebook groups and apps like Nextdoor, a private social network for your neighborhood. The downside to these options is that upon becoming a part of a social community, you will receive all the local information, contributions, and criticisms of your fellow neighbors. Such is the unfortunate nature of social media.

Once a young girl has found a job they are interested in, the interview process follows. Interview skills are also not quickly ingrained in our children. I haven't seen these skills taught or discussed in elementary school or middle school. If they are taught at all, it tends to be in high school, by which time most kids have already begun to earn their first dollars.

As these opportunities arise, it's essential to discuss first why good interview skills matter. Girls need to stand out from others for great job opportunities that have many applicants. Review what good interview skills look like, covering key discussion points such as appropriate manners, body language, attire, and whether they need to bring anything such as references or a résumé. Have your daughter practice with a mock interview with you before meeting with the potential employer. What questions might they ask, and what good questions can they ask the interviewer? Ultimately, she needs to prove her value and work ethic in relation to the opportunity.

LOSING CONFIDENCE

As much as earning money can build financial confidence in a girl, losing it can be equally devastating. One woman shared with me the memory of her drunk father taking her communion money when she was seven years old. It was so traumatic for her that she has never felt confident in her finances ever since. Even today as she's approaching retirement, she constantly worries about money. I bring this up because this is common among not only women but all adults. A lot of the worry and anxiety experienced by adults can be traced back to an experience from childhood. As parents, we need to be conscious of these potential long-term effects on children, even if they may not seem significant at the time.

Girls begin to decide how they want to earn money at an early age, earlier than most parents expect. It's an exciting time to watch your daughter plan and prepare how she wants to make money. This is the time that they begin to develop their negotiation skills and develop their value proposition to employers. As empowering as this time can be, there are also experiences that create negative emotions toward money in the long term.

8

Teaching Girls About Spending

Never spend your money before you have it.
–Thomas Jefferson

Just because someone is successful at earning money does not mean they will be wise in how they spend it. We see this in all adults, regardless of sex, age, and income level. Some of the early financial lessons girls receive are around spending. They are gifted money for their birthday and want to spend it on candy or a toy. Our spending patterns develop over time based on our desires, values, and emotions. For this reason, girls' experiences at a young age and their mindsets are crucial. Learning to control how we spend is one of the more critical pieces to managing our finances.

At a young age, children cannot make their own spending decisions. This quickly changes as they are allowed the independence to go out and choose what they can buy. For my girls, these decisions began when they started earning their allowance. Most of this early spending was on candy. It's still hard for me as a mom not to be critical and voice my opinion when I disagree with how they spend their money. Below are some ways to create better spending patterns at an early age.

WANTS VERSUS NEEDS

The first way is the concept of *wants versus needs*. When shopping, let your girls know what the purpose of the visit is as you enter a store. Discuss what you need from the store and tell them that you are not buying anything else. Ask questions aloud, "Is this something that we want? Do we need this item?" This exercise is not meant to suggest that we can only buy what we need. Instead, it helps girls understand that there is a difference between wants and needs, and prioritize between them. They cannot purchase everything that they want.

Another idea is to create games to help them understand the difference between wants and needs. When driving, watching TV, or shopping, ask them to identify whether a product is a need or want for the family. Family needs are buying food and gas and paying the electric bill; going out to the movies is a want. These simple points should be obvious to adults, yet these early discussions are essential for girls. It will help them prioritize their purchases as they get older when these decisions become more difficult (and expensive) to navigate.

Learning that they have to wait for something they want can be a tricky concept at times, but an important one. They may want a treat or toy and not have enough money. These girls at this young age can be persuasive, even cute, as they beg and plead for what they want. Do not be inconsistent and send mixed messages. If you make a rule, stick to it, and do not waiver. When kids want something, they will nag… a lot! Whenever your child asks for something, it's helpful to have a plan in place with your spouse or partner regarding how to respond. If you do not have a plan, the kids will eventually learn to manipulate the two of you to get what they want.

Sidney is excellent at this task. When she wants something, she approaches either my husband or me, never both of us. If she does not like the answer she hears, she will go to the other parent with the same request. Admittedly, she has had some success with this. Especially if she sees us busy at work with something else and we are distracted. Be aware that this is intentional and this behavior can start at a very young age.

Responding to this behavior is easier said than done, I realize. As persuasive as these girls can be, don't give in. I've done this on occasion, and when they're young, it seems cute and innocent, but later in life, it is no longer cute if these habits persist. If you have watched the movie *Vacation*, then you are familiar with Cousin Eddie, played by Randy Quaid. As funny of a character as he is, his financial sense is clearly missing. The position of an adult family member asking another for money is no longer cute.

WE DON'T HAVE ENOUGH MONEY FOR TODAY

Kaltrina Riley is the head of marketing for a global human resources business. She has three children under the age of four and shared with me how she discusses spending with her toddlers. They often visit a local gelato shop and toy store that are near each other. She will set the tone with her four-year-old son, who loves trucks, that they can look at the trucks but are not there that day to buy any. "Remember what I said? We don't have money for today." She explains that they receive money from their job to pay the bills and buy food (including the chicken nuggets he loves).

With the money left over, they decide how to spend it, by going on a trip, or purchasing gelato or a truck. She joked that this might be more extreme than other parents, but when I asked if she thought it worked, her response was, "My son doesn't say much initially, but then he will come back and ask questions, so I know he's listening." She then joked that when he goes to his grandparents, he will announce to them, "My mom doesn't have money to buy me a truck today, can you?" It sounds like he might be listening.

VALUE OF A DOLLAR

Teaching the value of a dollar in real-time is essential to financial knowledge. These lessons can be during day-to-day chores when you are out shopping. In the supermarket, give your girl a few dollars and ask her to pick which cereal, fruit, or ice cream to buy. Let her sort through the options, review the prices, and include them in the decision.

Follow through and purchase the item, letting her enjoy the decision. If you choose one thing over another, share with her why. If they are similar in quality and one is cheaper, relay that. After the purchase, show her the receipt—one purchased item may not seem like a lot, but a cartful of groceries, say $100, will be more impactful. Whenever I have brought my girls to Costco or BJ's, they are always surprised by how much we spend with a cartful of food.

My girls love ordering drinks from Starbucks. One of their favorites is the Grande Mango Dragonfruit Lemonade Refreshers beverage with light ice. This love shifted once they became responsible for buying these with their allowance. Kaylin quickly realized that these drinks could get pricey. She now considers these drinks a treat and has admitted that buying drinks at Dunkin Donuts (which she also enjoys) is cheaper.

DECORATING BEDROOMS

Courtney Maunsell is a senior vice president at a tech company. She decided to use a move to a new home as a teaching moment for her girls when they were eight and ten. She wanted them to be able to decorate their rooms the way that they wanted. They were each given a budget for the room. "We felt like giving them a budget was a good life lesson."

Each girl handled the budget differently. The younger daughter focused on bedding, pillows, and a futon. She didn't spend every last penny, while the older one did. The older girl bought a bed frame, a rug, end tables, and new bedding. She spent a lot of time online figuring out where she could get the best deals. She understood how stores would have sales throughout different parts of the year and took advantage of Labor Day sales. As a parent, it is exciting to watch each girl form her values and make her own decisions.

As these girls begin to spend and build their independence, they will need guidance through this learning process. It starts with differentiating wants versus needs and learning the value of a dollar. Incorporate this into your family life and give each girl the space to create her own perspective.

9

Teaching Girls About Savings

Do not save what is left after spending,
but spend what is left after saving.

—Warren Buffett

Saving is often the most complex and frustrating aspect of managing money. Most adults admit feeling that they never saved enough and wishing they would have started earlier. This lack of planning is a reason that so many adults are stressed and have anxiety.

We must introduce this to kids at a young age, especially girls. As we've discussed, women are likely to live longer than men. There is also a 50% chance women will end up in a divorce. Women are also more likely to leave the workforce to care for a family member, say a child or parent. By going, they may walk away from a retirement plan or income the government uses to calculate their social security. Women will rely more on their savings with any of these potential outcomes. Therefore, we must prepare them for this.

Saving goes back to the fundamental discussion of wants and needs. Remember Sam Renick, founder of Sammy Rabbit Money School in Chapter 5? Saving, he describes, teaches kids how to delay gratification. "It asks you to wait for something possibly better." When girls are young, their wants are small. Early on with my girls, it was Robux points or a bag of candy. Giving it to them without a second thought is easy as a parent.

Yet there are long-term consequences to keep in mind. As girls get older, these wants become more expensive. I recall the first request I received for an American Girl doll. As if the doll wasn't expensive enough, you also need to buy clothes and accessories for her. One weekend, I passed a garage sale where a woman was selling all her American Girl doll clothes and a bedroom set in a bundle for one price. Doug did the negotiating as he was the only one with cash in his wallet. He was completely unaware of what this would all cost, brand new. I even googled it on my phone as he tried to negotiate a price. Doug was apprehensive but settled on $80 for these used clothes and a bedroom set. The sticker shock of what girls want will come quickly.

Sidney recently sent me a birthday wish list she created on the Lululemon app. At the time, I wasn't even aware that she knew they had an app. Her list included 16 items and totaled $1,297! She didn't expect me to get her all of it (at least that's what she told me), but the wants get pricey quickly. And, I'm sorry to say that this trend will continue—before long, they'll start talking about a car.

PIGGY BANK

Create an actionable way to save. It becomes more difficult in a cashless world, but piggy banks are a great way to teach saving. Create an activity with these girls where they drop their saved coins into the piggy bank. This simple act, where they hear the clink of their coins in the jar, can create a powerful memory. Many adults have shared this tactic with me as we have discussed how they saved money growing up.

The goal is to associate savings with a sense of accomplishment and incentivize your girls to want to save more. If the piggy bank is dedicated to a specific want, research the cost with them and create a savings plan. Every time she contributes to the plan, help her count how much she has and how much more she needs to achieve her goal. If she consistently puts money in the piggy bank, discuss how long it will take her to reach her destination. If she is not happy with the timing of achieving this goal, how can she change the savings process?

Instead of using just one piggy bank, consider using two or three. I lost track of how many piggy banks my girls received as gifts when they were young. You can also keep it simple by using jars where they can use their artistic abilities and decorate them. Label the jars: SPEND, SAVE, and GIVE. If you do not want to use physical cash, consider play money or a jar of marbles. In place of piggy banks and jars, you can draw a chart on a posterboard to track savings. The options are endless. The goal is to create a process these girls can visualize and participate in.

BUDGETS

As a financial advisor, I am amazed by how many adults admit they do not have a budget. These piggy banks, jars, or charts are the first steps in the timeless lesson of budgets. Determine how you want your girl to allocate money to her SPEND, SAVE, and GIVE jars. Allocate the corresponding percentage into each category whenever she receives money. If the family is working toward a goal, such as a summer vacation, use a savings jar to plan toward this goal. Place it in a location where the entire family can participate.

Ensure your girl's goal is not too pricey so that they do not get frustrated. If they choose an expensive goal, you can always create a matching program and contribute a dollar for each dollar they save. The earlier you begin this process, the less resistance you will have. These girls will not know any different. *And*, if they save up front, they will never miss the money.

Many Americans today live in massive debt because they did not learn how to implement a budget. If girls can create this habit early and enforce it as they age, they will have more control over their savings and debt, and save with more confidence.

PENNY SAVING CHALLENGE

One popular way to teach girls about saving is the *Penny Saving Challenge*. There are various ways to do this challenge. The most common way is to start by saving one penny on the first day of the challenge. Each day you add one cent to the amount you saved the day before. By day 365, they will have saved $667.95.

There are endless charts you can buy and download to assist you with this challenge. Other options are a 52-week challenge and even a 30-day challenge. Ultimately the goal of each challenge is to teach girls discipline around saving. Every day they will thoughtfully save their money and watch their cents grow into hundreds of dollars over time.

Patience is key; money does not grow overnight. Patience is an essential trait as it relates to savings. It is not easy to delay gratification. It is necessary for your girls to plan and wait for the expensive items they want to buy. By practicing this, they create self-discipline that should serve them well as they save for larger expenses, such as a car, college, a home, or even retirement.

75%

Ali Caravella is the founder of a coaching business. The idea of 75% was instilled in Ali at an early age by her mother. This meant that for any money she received or earned, she would keep only 75%, putting the rest towards savings. For example, when her grandmother would give Ali money, her mother would walk her into a bank and deposit the remaining 25% into a passbook savings account. With the evolution of online banking and savings, these are a thing of the past, but this habit of Ali's is not. She continues to live by 75% and claims, "If you save up front, you never miss the money."

WHAT IF?

So many adults constantly worry and think, "What if– happens?" From speaking to women about investing, I have found those who developed money habits at a young age tend to pass them on to their children. I also have learned that women who experience financial challenges at a young age often pass on positive habits to their kids.

One woman I spoke with experienced bankruptcy due to health care costs when she was a teenager. Her mom was diagnosed with ovarian cancer and unfortunately passed away. This misfortune shaped her path towards a successful career in health care, and today she believes in teaching her six- and eight-year-olds the importance of saving at an early age.

She does this by physically showing her kids the money they earn through performing chores or certain projects. She also takes them to the bank and will match their earnings by pulling out the same amount. She comments, "When I'm really prepared, I'll take that money and turn it into $1 bills in advance so they physically see the pile of money." That's an experience I can't imagine her kids will forget.

EIGHTH WONDER OF THE WORLD

Time is one of the most powerful tools in investing. The reason for this is what the industry refers to as compound interest. Albert Einstein once said, "Compound interest is the eighth wonder of the world. He who understands it, earns it. He who doesn't pays it." Think of this concept as a snowball effect, meaning that as your investment grows, it grows exponentially larger with each addition. Or as Benjamin Franklin describes, "Money makes money. And the money that money makes, makes money."

For example, if you invest for 25 years with a 10% return, many might assume that over that period you would earn 250% (25 years x 10%). With the power of compound interest, the interest will earn more interest, so that instead of earning a 250% return, you'll earn 985%. That 735% makes a huge difference.

Figure 1 below illustrates how various rates of return and compounding over time can affect an investment account. The example examines a $1,000 investment over a 10-year period that grows at three different rates of return: 1%, 5%, and 10%. the bottom line shows a 1% rate of return (possibly a savings account) and over 10 years, grows to $1,105. the middle line shows a 5% rate of return, exhibiting more interest compounding and growth compared to the 1%, and resulting in $1,647 over 10 years. Finally, the top line shows a rate of 10%; notice the much wider growth rate between the 5% and 10% is than between the 1% and 5%. At a 10% rate the $1,000 grows to $2,707 over 10 years. Again, this is a simple $1,000 over 10 years. Imagine how this chart grows with larger investments and longer periods of time. Now imagine the power of a ten-year-old girl, retiring at age seventy and saving for 60 years.

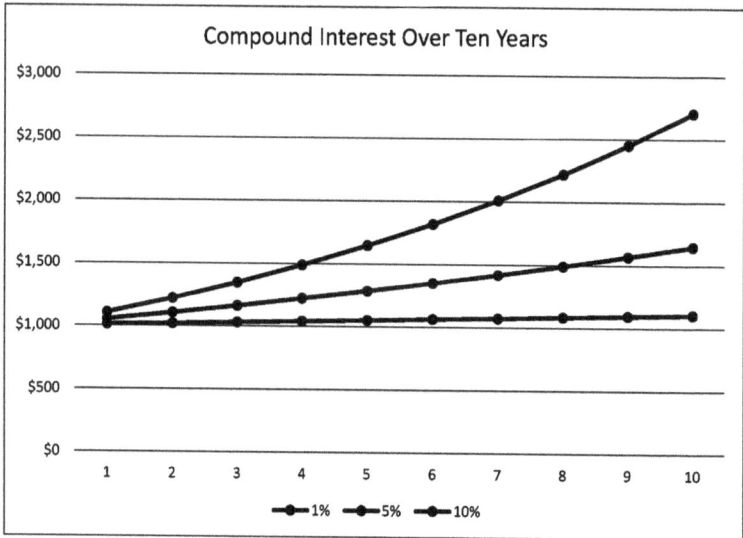

Figure 1.

The longer you invest those returns, the more dramatic the effect. This is why you want to start investing as early as possible. As Einstein so eloquently states, it can be detrimental to your savings if you don't understand and utilize this. So, help your girl start saving early, even if it's a small amount. This will create a consistent savings habit for her.

The other key to compound interest is to not touch it once it's set up. Charlie Munger is the vice chairman of Berkshire Hathaway and is known as the right-hand man to Warren Buffett. He recommends, "The first rule of compounding is to never interrupt it unnecessarily." The snowball effect of compound interest can't work if the interest is not reinvested. Therefore, it can't grow at the accelerated rate that we discussed. Time and patience are the drivers of this success.

BEANIE BABIES

One example of successfully saving at a young age is from Lindsay Ault-Authier, who started saving at ten by collecting quarters. When she had $5, she opened a savings account at her local bank. Her allowance at the time was $5 per week, and she desperately wanted Beanie Babies, which at the time were $6.99. Since her allowance was not enough to pay for these, she began a business: BAL, which stands for Basic Animal Lovers. She offered $2.50 per dog walk or $5 for the day. She even created a logo design and invoices for her customers.

Her planning and confidence continued; as an adult, her expectation was to "never have a man or anyone pay for me." She began investing in a 401(k) right out of school and shared her finances with her husband when she married. She now teaches responsibility in earning to her daughter. I neglected to ask her in my interview if she kept the Beanie Babies. Some of the rarest Beanie Babies today sell for thousands of dollars.

10
Teaching Girls About Investing

In investing, what is comfortable is rarely profitable.
—Robert Arnott

It is common for anyone to be overwhelmed when it comes to investing, including adults. And with good reason. As discussed in the last chapter, most adults admit to not saving enough money. The same holds for investing. Most adults admit to not feeling confident in their investing, and this is especially true of women. Women need to begin at a young age to invest with confidence going forward.

The definition of investing is to create and build wealth. There is an opportunity for a higher return, but with that comes risk. Investing is different from saving, where the purpose is preservation. Investing is growing your money for future needs and wants. For this reason, it is an essential building block to financial literacy. There are two concepts as they approach their teen years that create the building blocks of investing: stock ownership and the relationship between time and returns.

STOCK OWNERSHIP

Owning stocks over time has historically generated a more significant return versus bonds and cash... a lot more. With this higher return comes more risk over time. The potential for loss in owning stock is essential to recognize and requires patience. This lesson takes time, and every child and adult learns this at a different pace.

When you buy a stock, you own a piece of the company that issues it. You make money if the company does well and the share price increases, or you lose money if they don't do well. For example, if you buy 10 shares of a stock for $10 and the price increases to $15, your $100 investment is now worth $150. If the same stock instead falls to $5, your $100 investment is now worth only $50. You can make more money, but you can also lose it. This potential loss is the risk of investing. As parents, we must guide our girls through the experiences of loss. We must also teach them when and where it's appropriate to take these risks.

AT&T

There are many fun ways to engage girls in investing concepts. Most often, at this early age, the parents or other loved ones are investing money on behalf of the girls. Vivianne Kaneff's mother gifted her AT&T stock when she was six. She didn't quite grasp the idea of investing until one day, she found herself harassing her mother about buying something frivolous. The response from her mother was that she could pay for it, but to do that, she would have to sell some of her stock. Although this was not a good decision, and her mother knew it, she put it in Vivianne's hands. Vivianne realized this was not a good idea and chose not to sell the stock. When I asked her what she had wanted to buy, she joked that she could not even remember.

AMAZON

One way for girls to begin investing is through a Uniform Transfers to Minors Act (UTMA) account (more on this later). Doug and I did this for each of our girls. Some of this money, initially, were contributions from us. As the girls got older, we began to allocate some savings from their allowance into these accounts. We wanted to include them in the process and asked them to pick one company they believed would grow over time. The remainder of the investment decisions fell to us as the parents.

I asked Sidney, then nine, "If there was one company you would want to buy that you believe will continue to grow, what would it be?" Her answer was an adamant "Amazon. Mom, there's a box on our door every day from them."

Now again, there is only one share of Amazon in her account, but Sidney's experience in building confidence and a rationale for her investment selection is what's important. I am working with her to follow the price of Amazon in her account. I want to show her that prices go up and down. All investors need to be comfortable with this volatility concept to grow their money in the stock market.

FORD

Another story about investing comes from Meg Streck, who set up a Greenlight account (also explained later) to pay her kids their allowance, money earned, and to invest some of this money. She and her husband decided to allocate 60% of the money toward spending and

40% to savings. For the savings, they agreed that their kids would invest in the stock market. They began by giving each child seed money for the investing piece and explained, "We want you to go and research companies that you're interested in and come back to us, and we'll talk about buying that stock."

One of them, age nine, decided to invest in Ford because he read they were developing an electric truck. He explained, "They are going to try and be the American company that creates electric trucks, so I want to invest in them." So, his parents approved the purchase of the Ford stock.

With technology today, it's easy to monitor the price of a stock. He could watch the performance every day on the Greenlight app. One day he got frustrated because the stock went down. As this was occurring, I happened to be with his parents eating lunch. Our kids were together in a ski race program. It turns out he was on a ski lift looking at the stock price, became frustrated, and decided to try and sell it. His mom received an alert while we were eating and was able to stop the sale of the stock.

One of the app's benefits is it can manage the actions of a nine-year-old trading stocks on a ski lift, allowing the parents to follow up with a conversation. They told him, "You're not a day trader; these are long-term decisions you have to make here." She explained to me that at one point, his stock doubled, and then it went down. "It's been good for him to watch what has happened with the market and to understand that the market can sometimes be really good. And there's a flip side to the coin. You've gotta ride that out."

A final note to this story. These parents have two boys and no girls. I asked Meg if she had girls, would she have done the same thing? Her response was, "Absolutely!"

There are several important lessons in all of these stories. Allow girls to make an investment decision of their own, even if it is a small one. Create guardrails to control some of their investment decisions. Finally, engage them in their decision and the progress of their investment. Most kids, including my own, may not pick it up right away or even be interested. As I constantly do, keep trying.

Over time, these girls will understand and increase their knowledge about different types of companies. They will learn that many variables make these stocks go up and down. As you spend time deciding what stock to buy, you will experience just how many options there are. Stocks vary by sector, size, geography, and style. As complex as investing may appear, start simple. Over time their knowledge and investing experience will expand and benefit them tremendously.

BAKING

Stock ownership is one concept; another is understanding the relationship between time and return on investments. My girls and nieces have all learned how to bake over the years. Some love it more than others, but they know the fundamentals. Like anything, it can be overwhelming to follow a recipe, measure ingredients, and use an oven for the first time. Over time, the more you bake, the better the outcome. My niece Abby is an avid baker. When she was twelve, I interviewed her for my podcast. One of the questions I asked her was, "Why do you follow a recipe?"

Her response was, "I think following a recipe is important because it lets you know what you have to do. That way, it turns out the way you want it."

That answer seems so simple; so, apply it to investing. A recipe has a few fundamentals: ingredients, measurements, and time and temperature. Investing also has a few fundamentals: asset classes, allocation, and time and return.

The first fundamental, asset class, comprises stocks, bonds, and cash. Many girls are introduced to cash when they receive gifts and allowance, or start earning money. As we just discussed, the next step is to introduce stocks and how they work. It might be too early at this age to introduce bonds, which will come later as your girls start to understand loans and debt.

The second fundamental is the allocation to each asset class. In other words, determining the percentage of your money that goes to cash, stocks, and bonds. These girls are too young to make these decisions independently, but it's important to introduce them to the concept. If they already have piggy banks, savings jars, or other methods of dividing their money at a young age, this concept should not be new to them, but a continuation of their learning process. Additionally, when they decide how much to save versus how much to spend, these are also allocation decisions for their money.

This process formalizes as they reach their teens and want to start saving for more expensive items. These decisions early on will help them when it's time to begin saving and investing on their own. They will build on the good habits you have helped them create along the way.

RULE OF 72

The factors of time and return in investing are like the third funda-mental in baking, time and temperature. In baking, it's important to find the balance between the time you bake something and the temperature you bake it at. You don't want to underbake it, yet you don't want to burn it either. In investing, it's the amount of time required to reach your goal (known as time horizon), and the return you expect to achieve. The longer your time horizon, the greater probability of achieving a higher return.

Many adults struggle with this balance of time and return. To introduce the idea, I recommend the *Rule of 72* as a simple rule of thumb to teach girls about investing. It's a guide to tell you how long it will take to grow your investments. To calculate this, you take 72 and divide it by the assumed rate of return that your investment will grow. Doing this will tell you how long it will take to double your money.

Years to double your money = 72 divided by an assumed rate of return

For example, say you expect a return of 8%. If you divide 72 by 8, your money will double in 9 years. If you assume a lower rate of return, say 4%, 72 divided by 4 says that you will double your money in 18 years. The chart below highlights 5 rates of return: 1%, 2%, 4%, 6%, and 8%. Based on these returns, the bars show you how long it will take to double your money. You will notice a difference within these return ranges from over 70 to under 10 years. The higher the return, the quicker your investment will double.

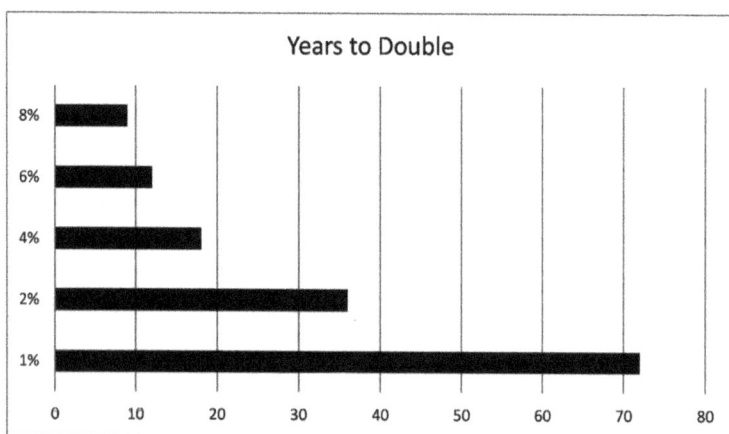

Years to Double

Rate	Years
8%	9
6%	12
4%	18
2%	36
1%	72

Figure 2.

Part 3

Actions For Financial Empowerment

11

Creating An Allowance

*Financial literacy is a very fancy term for saying spend it
smart, don't blow it, save what you can,
and know how the economy works.*

—Bill Clinton

Allowance is the most common tool to teach children how to manage money. It is a financial plan for kids. Of all the tools, I have found this topic one of the most debated among parents. What is allowance based on? Chores, grades, or nothing? How do you determine how much to pay? How often do you pay? Do you oversee their spending decisions, and if so, by how much? These are all fair questions with no easy answer.

GUIDELINES

Managing an allowance can create arguments between your girls and spouse or partner. With endless ways to approach this, here are some guidelines to consider when choosing the appropriate method for you and your family. These guidelines are essential to make this a positive learning experience rather than the cause of arguments. Trust me, I learned the hard way.

- *Determine an Appropriate Amount*

    Determining how much to give in an allowance is a bit of a balancing act. You want to pay your girls enough that they are making decisions about daily spending and long-term saving. Yet you do not want to give them so much money that they become careless. The amount must be age-appropriate. My rule of thumb was that I never wanted to be the parent with the highest or lowest allowance given to the child. While in elementary school, I paid my girls a weekly rate based on their current age. When my girls were ten, they received $10.

    When we started the allowance process, my sister and I were struck by how the allowance rates varied based on where we lived. While I was paying $8 to my eight-year-old daughter at the time, the going rate where my sister lived was $20. Despite the difference for each girl, we were each comfortable with our allowance rate relative to our friends. Communication with other parents during this time can help you determine an amount you will be satisfied with.

- *Remain Consistent in Your Payments*

    It can be challenging to remain consistent in how you pay these girls. I struggled with paying my girls on time. My girls constantly argued with me about whether I forgot to pay them for the week or the last few weeks. I now keep a journal detailing when and how much I pay them. As your girls get older and you start electronically sending them money, this process gets easier. Tracking this will end any argument about how much you owe them.

Another aspect of consistency to pay attention to is ensuring that the allowance you pay one child at a certain age is the same for another at that same age. By paying my girls each week an amount based on their age, I ensured that my youngest daughter received the same allowance as her older sister had during the same period. Whether you agree with the dollar amount or not, it was a simple rule that they could not argue with.

- *Guide Them*

Set some rules that they need to follow. One rule example is that they cannot go and spend all of their allowance in one day, or they cannot spend it all in one place. Sidney would spend it all at Cumberland Farm on candy and slushies and Kaylin at Starbucks if they could! While these girls need to know that this is their money and they are free to choose how they spend it, do not give them complete independence.

An idea that I implemented when I started to journal their allowance was an automatic savings plan for each girl. Each week when they get paid their allowance, a portion is held in a savings bucket. The girls cannot touch the savings bucket, and I show them how this money is growing (or not) in their investment.

- *Plan and Communicate What Is Not in an Allowance*

This last guideline is often tricky but can once again alleviate arguments around allowance. Parents should plan and communicate what they will provide outside of the allowance, especially as the girls get older and spend more time socializing outside the home with their friends. Is it the parents' responsibility to pay for ice cream that the girls buy when walking home from school with friends? What about if the girls go to an amusement park or movie with friends? Are there special events or circumstances you would not include in an allowance? For example, we do not include in their allowance any birthday gifts they would need to buy for family and friends. All of these considerations can lead to potential debates. Once decided, communicate this in advance to your girls.

CHORES

One popular way to pay allowance is on a job-by-job basis. Emptying the dishwasher, vacuuming the house, feeding the dogs, and taking out the trash are all common examples. Some parents only pay their girls with this method, while others will complement the weekly allowance with specific jobs. When saving for something specific, my girls often ask for additional jobs and want to accelerate the savings process. Some of the more common chores in my family that we pay extra for include washing the car, sorting recyclables, and seasonal jobs such as stacking wood for the winter and moving the outdoor furniture in or out of the house.

CLOTHING ALLOWANCE

For girls, considering a clothing allowance is important as they approach their teenage years. I grew up on one and implemented it for my oldest daughter in middle school. Some may argue against a clothing allowance, believing that we should buy clothes for our children as we do any other necessity. But I believe it should be based on what she wants to buy.

Girls today want clothing from brands like Lululemon and Aviator Nation. Tomorrow they may want clothes from somewhere else; regardless, it will still be pricey. I cannot believe how often I have told my girls, "I would never buy that for myself!"

There are several ways to implement a clothing allowance. One option is to have a predetermined amount of money set aside for clothes. The idea is to create a baseline where if the girls want designer clothing or shoes, they either pay for it or contribute to the cost. For example, let's say they want to buy $130 leggings, and you decide a fair value is $40, should they make up or contribute to the $90 difference? What if you determine shoes are valued at $50, and they want a new pair of Converse that cost $150? Often, I see adults not make these pricing decisions until their child asks them to purchase the item. Not determining this ahead may become problematic as the child will likely disagree on the amount that you decide is fair.

My sister chose a slightly different approach. Her girls have school uniforms, so she buys their "staples," including school- and weekend-related basics. She then gives them an allowance for the "lulu" decisions. This process has worked for her family, and each of her girls thoughtfully plans how to allocate their dollars. As I write this book, we are preparing for a beach vacation together. All four of our girls have spent hours over FaceTime preparing what they have saved up to purchase.

A last option, not as commonly used, is one that I use with my oldest daughter. My sister and I had this allowance growing up. We received a monthly allowance for all our clothes and were responsible for all our purchases. This allowance did not include winter jackets, formal dresses, and essential shoes. I never felt that the allowance was enough; like my girls today, there was always some pricey item that I wanted to purchase. The process of planning and saving for an expensive item is why I appreciate the method today.

Kaylin was initially excited about this allowance and the independence she was receiving to purchase her clothes. She immediately bought Lululemon leggings, then quickly realized the limitations of her money, particularly when the seasons changed and she had outgrown her clothes from the last season. Admittedly, we have had to tweak the dollar amount along the way, but overall, this method works for us.

GRADES

Using grades as a basis for determining allowance is another consideration for parents. Vicki Whalen, who retired after a successful career in finance, paid an allowance to her boys not based on chores but grades. She began this method in middle school, and it's still ongoing for them now in high school. They predetermined an amount for each grade the boys received and the type of class that it was. For example, grades in gym class were not considered part of their allowance, only the core classes were.

50 CENTS

Some parents will also consider penalizing their girls through their allowance. My mother did just that to my sister and me growing up. Two things that drove my mother crazy were when we said "like" or slammed her car door. Anytime we used those phrases or slammed her door, she deducted 50 cents from our allowance. I can still hear her yelling, "That's 50 cents!" Some weeks I ended up with no money. I want to think that this worked at least two-thirds of the time. I do not slam car doors or use the phrase "like" to this day. Looking back, I wish that "um" had been part of this penalty. Unfortunately, to this day, I still say "um" too much.

TOKEN SYSTEM

Managing the use of screen time with kids is a challenge for all parents. I am amazed today by how many kids are on their phones or tablets when eating at a restaurant. It is a constant battle with my girls that I admit to not monitoring as well as I would like.

The *token system* is a method I learned about as I was writing this book, and I wish I had heard about it years ago. The strategy is to use a token, which can be anything visible and countable as an incentive for a child to complete a specific task or behavior. One way to use this starts with giving a child 10 tokens at the beginning of the week. Each child has to decide each week how to use these tokens. They can exchange the tokens for either 30 minutes of screen time or 50 cents. If they choose only one of the two, this will add up to either $5 or 5 hours of screen time at the end of the week. Certainly, the amount of screen time and payment can be revised based on the child's age. This author even added onto this system, where if the child read for 30 minutes, they would receive an additional token for this task. He describes the results as "incredible" and reported that reading time for his child went up and screen time went down by 90%. He suggests that the key to this system is to start small, encourage progress, and celebrate small wins (McKeown 2014).

FAMILY MOMENTS

One last idea on this subject is not an alternative to our discussed options but a fun way to involve the kids in family moments. Several women have told me they will include the kids in planning for a large vacation. This involves creating and sharing a budget, allowing them to engage in what activities they want to include on their vacation, where they want to stay, and for how long.

Allowance is a powerful tool to guide girls in their financial decisions. They will learn to plan, build discipline, and ultimately create a sense of independence. Families should start with their own budget and evaluate what they are comfortable with in determining an allowance. There is no perfect answer to an allowance, they will be customized to suit the family's needs.

The building blocks of money and finance (earning, spending, saving, and investing) start at a young age and evolve over time. Allowance is a method used by most parents to teach these money building blocks to their children in real time. There are also tools that parents can use, and these continue to evolve. Today there are debit and prepaid cards, custodial accounts, 529 plans, and Coverdell Education Saving Accounts.

12
Using Debit And Prepaid Cards

Procrastination is like a credit card:
it's a lot of fun until you get the bill.

—Christopher Parker

As girls begin to purchase items independently, it's time to consider a debit or prepaid card. At a young age, children observe adults swiping cards at a checkout counter or a restaurant and quickly make the connection that a card is cash. The more difficult connection to understand is that these cards are not limitless. By managing their debit card, children will make the connection and learn that the money is limited.

There has been tremendous growth with debit cards and prepaid card options. Debit cards are linked to a custodial checking account, meaning an adult opens and manages an account for the child's benefit. As the child uses the card for purchases, or at an ATM, the amount charged is deducted from money in the checking account. With a prepaid card, parents can load it with money, typically from their account, for their child to spend. A prepaid card is not attached to a checking account, so the child can't take out more than what they have and incur a potential overdraft fee because they can't spend what's not there.

Overspending is an important lesson and stepping stone for kids before they own their first credit card. Credit card debt is a massive problem today and growing, especially as the cost of living continues to rise. This debt is one of many indicators of how many adults never learned how to properly manage their finances. Debit cards and prepaid cards will limit the mistakes girls can make with their spending habits at an early age. It also will allow them to create better habits than past generations.

If your child makes a financial mistake, it won't be that they overspent, but instead that they ran out of money. They will quickly realize their limitation on what they can purchase in the future. It teaches them that money is finite and that money spent today limits what they can spend tomorrow. When your child uses their card, the owner (adult) will automatically receive a notification as to the amount and location of the purchase. I have found it greatly beneficial to observe how and where they spend their money, as well as the habits they form. Walgreens is a clear giveaway to me that my girls are spending money on makeup and candy. Firehouse means ice cream, and Apricot Lane means jewelry, you get the point.

Try to fight the temptation of bailing them out when they run out of money. Easier said than done, I admit I've done it with my girls. A couple of dollars here or there may not seem like a lot, but eventually, these young girls can misunderstand the message. As they get older, it will no longer be a few dollars that they will need. We don't want to give them the impression that we will be there to rescue them from all their future mistakes.

Another benefit to these debit cards is they function as a payment and savings plan for children. Two such examples of these cards are Greenlight and Busy Kid. Once your bank account links to their card, money can be sent via an app to their card. You can use the app as a function of how much you pay them by assigning monetary value to chores they complete each day. Maybe it's 50 cents for emptying the dishwasher or $1 for emptying the trash. As the card owner, you can assign as many chores as you'd like. They suggest you create your own if you don't see one that you want to use. Another feature is that the adult owner and child can use the app to track the funds on the card, the chores completed, and the allowance earned (if you choose to use this function).

I think this is a fantastic tool. Unfortunately, the chores feature did not work with my family. We argued with our girls about what chores they completed each week. Whether they emptied the dishwasher on Monday, fed the dogs on Tuesday, or did their laundry on Wednesday. Instead, I transferred a weekly allowance to their card, assuming they earned it. These apps are flexible enough that you can find a process that works for your family.

Another feature of these cards is the saving and sharing feature. With the money sent to the card, you can decide how to allocate spending, saving, and giving. Using Busy Kid as an example, you can select from over 4,000 stocks and ETFs (Exchange Traded Funds) for investing. For giving, there are over 50 national and regional charities from which to choose. These girls have endless options to decide how they might want to save and give.

BACK TO FORD

In chapter 10, I shared the story of Meg and how her son invested in Ford. They paid their kids for their chores through the Greenlight app and allocated 40% of their money for savings. They selected Ford from thousands of available stocks and could track its performance. More importantly, Meg, as the account owner, received alerts when her son was using the card or trying to invest or sell something.

Some things to consider when deciding which card is appropriate for you include the fees associated with the account, the minimum dollar amount required, and the potential interest earned on the checking account. Look for customer-friendly mobile apps where parents can transfer money, see where their child spends it, set spending limits, and block specific merchants. The card features and fees vary by each issuer, including the minimum age of the child, which typically ranges from about six to thirteen. Make sure you research your options before deciding on the one that suits you best.

These cards have evolved over the years. There are now more controls on how young children manage their money. They can't overspend. Instead, they learn to budget their money and advance toward saving and giving. These are the building blocks of their long-term financial well-being.

13

The Benefits Of Custodial Accounts

Money is only a tool. It will take you wherever you wish, but it will not replace you as the driver.

—Ayn Rand

Custodial accounts are another option to consider as a vehicle for savings. These accounts are intended to hold gifts and assets that a minor receives, but they are owned and controlled by an adult until the child reaches the age of majority. This age is usually eighteen or twenty-one, depending on the state of residence.

The two custodial accounts options are the Uniform Gift to Minors Act (UGMA) and the Uniform Transfers to Minors Act (UTMA). Within these accounts, you grow your money through the investments you choose. Both can include assets such as stocks, bonds, and mutual funds. A UTMA can also include tangible assets such as real estate, jewelry, and art.

There are pros and cons to consider with custodial accounts. These accounts offer more flexibility on how to spend your money versus a 529 or a Coverdell account (discussed in the next chapter). The latter accounts are specifically designated for education. These accounts are easy to open for adults looking to make a gift to minors, and no trusts or special estate-planning documents are required. Large custodians such as Fidelity and Charles Schwab, money managers such as Vanguard, broker-dealers, and even robo-advisors offer these accounts through a simple, online process.

Another benefit of custodial accounts is the investment opportunity on behalf of these girls. My girls have a UTMA account for the money they save from their allowance. I share their statements with them on occasion to show them not only how much they have saved, but also to introduce them to investing. They have seen their investments both grow and lose value at times. This process is still new to us; I can confidently say that this is not an easy lesson for kids. It will take some time and repetition.

With custodial accounts, the child becomes the owner at the age of majority, regardless of their financial knowledge. While the kid may view this as a positive, the parents may disagree. The concern from parents is that the kid can now spend the money however they would like. They may choose to blow it all on a brand new, obscene car instead of making a wise decision to use it towards a necessity or a long-term goal. The less experience they have at this stage of managing money, the more likely they are to make a financial mistake. There are also some considerations to keep in mind regarding control, taxation, and financial aid.

CONTROL

First, transferring money into these accounts is considered an irrevocable gift—it can't be taken back. Although the adult acts as the account's custodian and may have current control over how the money is invested, the child is ultimately the owner. That means that the adult will have no control when their child reaches the age of majority, despite how the adult may want the child to handle their new money.

TAXATION

There are certain tax considerations to keep in mind regarding custodial accounts. The money transferred into these accounts is considered a gift, therefore, according to the Internal Revenue Service (IRS) for 2023, any gift above $17,000 will be subject to the gift tax. These accounts are also taxable, with the income and capital gains being taxed each year they are earned. This means that someone may have to pay taxes on this account. Known as the "Kiddie Tax," for the year 2023, no taxes were owed on the first $1,150 of unearned income, taxed at the child's rate on the next $1,100, and then above that at the parent's rate.

FINANCIAL AID

As for financial aid, keep in mind that these accounts may also impact a kid's eligibility when applying to college. For parents considering financial aid for their children, these accounts will be reported on the Free Application for Federal Student Aid (FAFSA) as an asset of the student. FAFSA is the federal form you must fill out to receive any financial aid from the government to help pay for college. As an asset to the student and not the parent, the federal financial aid formula will reduce eligibility by about 20% of the value of this account.

ROTH IRA

While most parents use custodial accounts as savings vehicles for their kids, a Roth IRA is also worth mentioning. Especially if you are concerned about financial aid, looking for a more efficient way to invest, and can allocate these savings toward retirement. A Roth IRA is an individual retirement account used for saving toward retirement.

As discussed in Chapter 9, time is one of the most powerful tools in investing. Time allows interest to compound and grow at an accelerated rate, which is why Albert Einstein described it as the eighth wonder of the world. I realize these girls' retirement may be the last thing on parents' minds, but every bit will go a long way.

Roth IRAs are tax efficient because once you contribute after-tax dollars to the Roth IRA, the contributions and earnings grow tax-free *and* can be withdrawn tax-free after they turn fifty-nine and a half. To open a Roth IRA, the child must have earned income, and the contributions to the Roth IRA cannot exceed that income. Meaning if the child earns $20 for mowing the lawn, you can't fund the Roth IRA with $100. Another benefit is that parents can also contribute to their child's Roth IRA as long as it doesn't exceed the child's earned income. As long as there is earned income, Uncle Sam doesn't care how it is funded.

Parents have several options to consider as a savings vehicle for their girls, whether it's a custodial account or possibly a Roth IRA. You will want to weigh the pros and cons of these options as they relate to control, taxation, and financial aid eligibility. With a Roth IRA, make sure that this money is designated for use when they are past the age of fifty-nine and a half.

14

Why Start College Planning Now

Education is the most powerful weapon which
you can use to change the world.

—Nelson Mandela

The last thing you want to think about when a child is born or even in their formative years is their future college education. Why would you, if you have 16 years? Every parent will say it goes by like the blink of an eye, and when it comes to this, you certainly want time on your side, meaning the earlier you can prepare financially, the better the outcome and the less stressful it will be.

Outside of a home purchase, this tends to be one of the most significant financial decisions a family can make. It will also be one of your life's most emotional financial decisions. The future success of your child relies heavily on their education. Studies show individuals are paid more the higher their degree. A bachelor's degree, on average, results in 88% higher pay than a high school degree. Even more, a professional degree results, on average, in 265% higher pay. (J.P. Morgan Asset Management, 2023)

Paying for college is getting more expensive each year, creating additional stress for families. A newborn today is expected to pay (including tuition, fees, room, and board) $241,168 for a public undergraduate degree and $554,220 for a private one. (J.P. Morgan Asset Management. 2023) Generally speaking, the cost of a private education is over double the price of a public one.

Part of the difficulty in addressing this early on is deciding how much should be financed toward their education. As a parent, do you want to support their entire education, none of it, or somewhere in between? Do you plan for private or public education? Unfortunately, as college costs rise, total financial aid has fallen. For families that lack the finances to fund college, the remaining option is to borrow the money. Student loan debt is the fastest growing of any other debt, more than auto, credit card, and home equity line of credit.

Even if parents can't or don't want to immediately make these decisions, looking at options early is wise. It's essential to understand what time can provide for this investment. The second is to understand the account options available specific to education.

TIME

Once again, let's address the importance of time when it comes to investing. There's an opportunity cost associated with every year you delay investing. The same principle applies to funding a college education.

Here's an example of a missed opportunity. Let's say you invest $350 a month in a tax-deferred account, assuming an investment return of 7%. If you begin investing when the child is born and have 18 years to invest, the accumulation will be $148,154. Suppose you wait just five years? Think about this. She isn't even in elementary school. How many families will wait this long before they think to invest in college? Now, with only 13 years left, the result is a difference of over $60,000, valued at $87,765. (Fidelity Advisor. 2023) Imagine how much more difficult this becomes when girls turn ten.

To make up for this lost opportunity, you will need to do one of two things. Either save more money or take out a loan. Most will agree that with today's cost of living, it's difficult for most to save more. Most choose the latter and take a loan, resulting today in an all-time high in student debt.

If you are reading this book, you are planning for the future of a young girl. I implore you to start this process now—don't wait. I even know professionals in finance that understand this philosophy. Despite this, they waited too long themselves and now regret it. Time moves fast, don't be one of them!

OPTIONS

Not only is the timing of this investment a vital consideration, but so is understanding the options specific to education savings. There are two types of plans: a 529 College Savings Plan and a Coverdell Education Plan. Here's a quick summary of both:

529 College Savings Plan

529 plans are tax-advantaged accounts, which means that while the money is in the account, the money grows tax-deferred, and no

taxes are due on the earnings. If the money is taken out for qualified education expenses, these withdrawals are tax-free. This means that there is no capital gains tax, ordinary income tax, or Medicare surtax from these withdrawals.

These plans are flexible on how they define a qualified education. At the college or graduate level, these funds can be used for tuition, books, supplies, and room and board for a full-time student at an accredited institution. Some plans include elementary school or high school. You can search for accredited schools by visiting the student aid website.

The structure of these accounts is that most often a parent, guardian, or grandparent opens the account and names a child as the beneficiary. Each plan is sponsored by an individual state, often with a financial services company (such as Fidelity, American Funds, or T. Rowe Price) managing the plan. You do not need to use the plan that is managed in the state you reside in. While there is no annual contribution limit to a 529, there are state-level limits on what qualifies for state tax credits or deductions. Some states don't offer any and some may limit the deduction to the plan that their state administers. With over a hundred plans today, make sure you understand the nuances of the plan you select.

Each program administrator imposes a maximum aggregate balance of all accounts per beneficiary, often $400,000 or more. For example, the maximum account balance for the State of New York in 2022 is $520,000. There are no income limits on the contributors nor age limits on the beneficiaries.

Unlike a custodial account that eventually transfers ownership to the child, the account owner in a 529 controls the assets and decides when and how to spend the money. An example of the flexibility is if the child does not use all the money, the owner can transfer the money to another beneficiary.

This alleviates a common concern about what happens if the student doesn't attend college or receives a scholarship. This money is transferable. Recent changes in federal law allow certain unused funds in a 529 Plan to be eligible to roll over into a Roth IRA for the same beneficiary (up to $35,000).

The investment options are another important feature of these plans. When you put money in a 529 account, the money does not, or should not, sit in cash. Every plan offers a range of mutual funds and has the flexibility to make investment changes, with most 529s, twice per calendar year or when you change beneficiaries.

A common question asked when considering a 529 plan is what happens if the money isn't used for education. In this case you will pay a 10% penalty and ordinary income taxes on the earnings (not the principal) if it does not qualify for education. As discussed, you can also transfer the account to another beneficiary that plans to use the funds for qualified education or rollover some of the assets to a Roth IRA. Also, if a child receives a scholarship and no longer needs these funds, you'll pay only the ordinary income taxes on the earnings of what you take out to offset the scholarship, not the penalty.

One of the most thoughtful financial decisions Doug and I made was to open a 529 account. We opened our plan about two months after Kaylin was born. We have been fortunate to take advantage of time. I worry about a lot of things; however, this one is no longer at the top of my list.

Coverdell Education Savings Account

Some parents may choose to utilize a Coverdell account, similar to a 529, which offers tax-free investing and withdrawals for qualified education expenses. Also similar to a 529, earnings on non-qualified withdrawals may be subject to a 10% penalty and federal, state, and local taxes. These accounts also tend to have a low impact on financial aid eligibility.

Unlike a 529, there are income limits on the contributors/parents. For 2023, joint filers with income of less than $190,000 can contribute up to the full amount. Contribution limits are lower at a higher income, and are completely phased out for joint filers with an income of $220,000 or more (Williams 2023). Furthermore, there is a maximum contribution of $2000 annually per beneficiary. Generally, one must contribute before the beneficiary reaches eighteen and use the assets by age thirty. In addition to college expenses, certain K–12 expenses are also considered qualified.

COMMUNICATION

Once you decide how you want to approach paying for education, communication with the child is essential. Admittedly, the elementary school years may be a bit early to have this discussion, but keep this in mind. At some point, when you discuss education with your girls, you will want to set expectations for them as to how they should think of their future education. If you plan to pay for part of their education, let them know what they will be responsible for. Some options to consider:

- You pay for room and board, and she pays for books and supplies.
- You pay for a public education, and she pays for the price difference if she decides to go to a private school.
- You pay for a percentage of the total education, say 50% or 75%.

Having this discussion with her sooner rather than later allows everyone to be on the same page and plan accordingly. It also mitigates family arguments when these expectations are clarified in advance. My brother-in-law has shared that after he graduated from high school, as he was packing to go to college, his stepfather approached him and asked, "How are you going to pay for college?" He had already been through the college application process, was accepted, and enrolled in a school. Why his father-in-law never felt compelled to ask him this earlier is appalling. But unfortunately, this happens to many people, and my brother-in-law was able to pivot, chart out a new path, and succeed on his own.

15

From Taboo To Empowerment

Communication can be such a simple act, yet there is evidence that finance is not discussed enough. With societal and demographic issues, this is crucial for women. You must talk about money with these girls and start young. We don't want them to think this is a taboo topic. Chuck Berke, PH.D., MCC, and D.O. of Berke Associates explains to me, "People would rather talk about their sex life than money." Women, in particular, admit that they have refrained from discussing money with family and friends. I find that rather disturbing, especially when most of these girls will look to their mothers or other women as role models.

Habits and the money mindset of individuals start at a young age. Children observe and hear everything you say and do, and this will shape their attitudes and values. These young girls are sponges; be aware of what you say and do in front of them.

PARENTAL BEHAVIOR

Parental behavior has a direct impact on the economic behavior of children. It can be overlooked during daily tasks and may not be noticeable, but values and principles slowly form. If you are a saver as a parent and articulate that to your children, there is an increased chance that they will continue that habit. The savings rate of parents versus their children has a significant positive association. (Webley, Paul and Nyhus, Ellen K. 2005) The more the parents save, the more likely their daughter will as well.

On the flip side, if you are not a saver and show these signs to your children, they will notice. Parents' habits are observed by their kids, even early on. And it's not just the action they absorb, it's the emotion along with it.

Decades of research show an increase in awareness of the habits and perceptions that manifest around money. Parents need to be more thoughtful of their messaging in front of their children, whether it's intentional or not. Be aware we also have a human tendency to find guidance from those similar to us. Girls will in particular pick these messages up from their mothers, grandmothers, teachers, and other influential women. Be careful what you say in front of your children. They observe and hear everything you say and do.

GOD DAMMIT, MOMMY!

My first realization of this was when my oldest, Kaylin, was three, and we were in a grocery store preparing for Thanksgiving. We were hosting 10 to 15 guests over the next couple of days and I had a long list with a mission to get everything in one shop. My daughter was anxious, couldn't stay seated in the cart, and managed to pull several items off the shelf as we walked by. I lost my patience as we turned a corner; she managed to pick up a plant and then drop it on the floor, destroying the plant and the pot that it was in. I was asked to leave. As mortifying as that was, I decided to take one more turn down an aisle in the hopes that I wouldn't have to return to the store over the holiday weekend.

The aisle was empty except for one elderly woman who slowly came toward us down the aisle. As her cart passed ours, my daughter decided to look me in the eye and say "God dammit, Mommy," and then turn and smile at the woman. I don't know what upset me more, the look on the woman's face or the pride that my daughter held in her comment. I never would have thought until that moment that she had heard me say that; maybe I assumed that she was so young that it wouldn't matter? Shame on me.

TURN SHARING INTO GIVING

Winston Churchill once said, "We make a living by what we get, but we make a life by what we give." It seems every generation says, "My children have more than I ever had growing up." It is a delicate balance we look for in raising our children. We want them to be better off than we might have been, yet instill in them that there is more to happiness than material goods. Parents want their children to be thoughtful and genuinely care for others, not just smart about how they manage money. Not only do we want to raise selfless children, but some studies show that giving improves happiness.

To give means that one has empathy. Girls can build empathy at a young age by sharing, which will develop their social connection to others and self-confidence as they grow. Sharing is an important lesson where kids can engage early on with simple tasks such as splitting things like pizza or ice cream and sharing a toy with another child or sibling. Talk to them when they share about their kindness and ask them how they feel about it.

As we have discussed earlier, these girls observe the acts of their parents and other adults around them. Allow them to experience it firsthand. Lead by example and show them how you share, why you do it, and how it makes you feel. Spend time with them discussing how you can help others, especially if an unforeseen event, such as a hurricane, has occurred. If you donate clothes or food to a local drive, have them participate by collecting and delivering the items.

The best tip I have received from parents is to observe and include your children's interests in this process. Back to the jar example, if they allocate money to SAVE, engage them on how they want to donate it. Give them the freedom to choose where the donation goes; let them deliver the donation in person if possible. Too often, we rely on online donations; I am certainly at fault for that, but think of the impact on them of delivering a donation in person. Suppose sharing becomes a natural part of their lives, and they learn how gratifying it is to be generous. In that case, they are more likely to grow into kind and giving adults where charitable giving will be inherently a part of them.

SODA AND PIZZA

One memory related to sharing is from Raechelle Minney when she was in second grade. Her father created a system where she would get paid $1 for her chores. With this dollar, she would buy a soda and pizza and always had enough to buy for a friend as well. Even as an adult today, she can recall how good she felt doing something for a friend.

None of these values or lessons we instill in them will resonate overnight. Sharing is simple for young girls, yet many will need encouragement. I asked my girls if they remembered sharing at a young age and how they felt. Both independently responded that they did not recall sharing. My older daughter replied, "I remember you and dad forcing me to share with my sister." It certainly was not the response I hoped for, yet it reminds me that this process takes time.

Yet over time, sharing will help them socialize and interact with friends, teach them about compromise and fairness, and help them feel rewarded by giving to others. On a larger scale, they will give back to their community as they get older. Many studies suggest that women donate more over time than men. Whether this donation is in dollars or time, it is essential to know that women are significant contributors to the world of giving.

FINAL THOUGHTS

The road to financial literacy takes a village and it takes time. As parents we question whether our actions are the most appropriate and effective—this is common. I hope that by sharing lessons I have learned from others, parents can decide for themselves what will be best for their girls. As crucial as it is to prepare girls to mature into women who can manage their own money, finances, investments, and savings, there is an even more meaningful impact. Through this process these girls create independence, which empowers them to grow with confidence, happiness, and empathy. What more could we wish for our girls?

Notes

Connect With Julina:

www.julinaogilvie.com

Podcast Women on Wealth

YouTube: @womenonwealthbywomenforwom5206

LinkedIn: https://www.linkedin.com/in/julina-ogilvie-cima%C2%AE-cpwa%C2%AE-90b12a11/

Acknowledgements

As a first-time author navigating the intimidating world of book creation, I found myself so fortunate to have an incredible network of people who stood by me every step of the way. I am humbled by the generosity of those friends and professionals who entrusted me with their stories—the stories that lie at the heart of this book. These narratives, filled with personal experiences, emotions, and decisions surrounding finance, have added depth and authenticity to the pages within. I am grateful to the hundreds of professionals who generously shared their time and stories during my interview process to allow for diverse perspectives.

A special thanks as well to the following contributors whose insights and narratives found a place in this book:

Lindsay Ault-Authier
Chuck Berke
Ali Caravella
Matt Gudonis
Vivianne Kaneff
Mary Ellen McGuire
Courtney Maunsell

Rachelle Minney
Judi Otton
Kaltrina Riley
Meg Streck
Dr. Patty Ann Tublin
Vicki Whalen

And finally, a special thanks to my family, friends, and colleagues who provided guidance and support. Your insights, advice, and willingness to lend an ear made the process feel less daunting. Your words of encouragement propelled me forward, I am deeply grateful. Thank you for being part of this journey.

With love and gratitude, Julina

About the Author

Julina Ogilvie, CIMA®, CPWA®
Partner | Wealth Advisor

Julina manages wealth for high-net-worth individuals and families at Principle Wealth Partners based in Connecticut. Prior to joining Principle Wealth Partners, she held executive roles at J.P. Morgan Asset Management and Lord Abbett & Co. In these roles, she used her extensive knowledge of the capital markets to educate the country's top advisors.

Julina is an accomplished speaker and strategist who has presented wealth management concepts to thousands of financial professionals and clients. She has been recognized for her outstanding achievements and serves as a mentor for young women entering the business. With a passion for financial literacy she created a podcast, *Women on Wealth*, to empower women on financial concepts.

Julina resides in Fairfield, CT with her husband Doug, their daughters Kaylin and Sidney, and two dogs Mudd and Sierra. She currently sits on the Ethics Board of the Investments & Wealth Institute, serves as VP of Finance at the Westport Women's Club, and serves on the Board of Directors for River House in Cos Cob, CT. Julina is an avid skier and triathlete who qualified for the USA Triathlon Age Group National Championships in 2022 and 2023, and the Ironman World Championship in 2024.

Education & Certifications:
Colgate University
Certified Investment Management Analyst®
Certified Private Wealth Advisor®

Featured in:
Citywire
Parents.com
MoneyGeek

Dear reader,

Thank you for reading this book and joining the Publish Your Purpose community! You are joining a special group of people who aim to make the world a better place.

What's Publish Your Purpose About?
Our mission is to elevate the voices often excluded from traditional publishing. We intentionally seek out authors and storytellers with diverse backgrounds, life experiences, and unique perspectives to publish books that will make an impact in the world.

Certified

(B)

Corporation

Beyond our books, we are focused on tangible, action-based change. As a woman- and LGBTQ+-owned company, we are committed to reducing inequality, lowering levels of poverty, creating a healthier environment, building stronger communities, and creating high-quality jobs with dignity and purpose.

As a Certified B Corporation, we use business as a force for good. We join a community of mission-driven companies building a more equitable, inclusive, and sustainable global economy. B Corporations must meet high standards of transparency, social and environmental performance, and accountability as determined by the nonprofit B Lab. The certification process is rigorous and ongoing (with a recertification requirement every three years).

How Do We Do This?
We intentionally partner with socially and economically disadvantaged businesses that meet our sustainability goals. We embrace and encourage our authors and employee's differences in race, age, color, disability, ethnicity, family or marital status, gender identity or expression, language, national origin, physical and mental ability, political affiliation, religion, sexual orientation, socio-economic status, veteran status, and other characteristics that make them unique.

Community is at the heart of everything we do—from our writing and publishing programs to contributing to social enterprise nonprofits like reSET (www.resetco.org) and our work in founding B Local Connecticut.

We are endlessly grateful to our authors, readers, and local community for being the driving force behind the equitable and sustainable world we are building together. To connect with us online, or publish with us, visit us at www.publishyourpurpose.com.

Elevating Your Voice,

Jenn T Grace

Jenn T. Grace
Founder, Publish Your Purpose

*9 7 9 8 8 8 7 9 7 0 8 2 0 *